# PRODUCTION FUNCTIONS

T5-BPY-598

*To Joanny*

# Production functions

**A theoretical and empirical study**

DEREK L. BOSWORTH

SAXON HOUSE | LEXINGTON BOOKS

© Derek L. Bosworth, 1976

All rights reserved. No part of this publication may be reproduced, stored in a retrieval system, or transmitted in any form or by any means, electronic, mechanical, photocopying, recording, or otherwise without the prior permission of D. C. Heath Ltd.

*Published by*
SAXON HOUSE, D.C. Heath Ltd.
Westmead, Farnborough, Hants., England


*Jointly with*
LEXINGTON BOOKS, D.C. Heath & Co.
Lexington, Mass. USA


ISBN   0 347 01122 5

Library of Congress Catalog Card Number   75–36966

Printed in Great Britain by
Robert MacLehose & Co. Ltd
Printers to the University of Glasgow

4B
241
B67

# Contents

200088

v

**Figures**

# Preface

I would like to thank everyone who helped directly or indirectly in the research contained in this book, particularly all of my friends who worked in the Manpower Unit in the Centre for Industrial Economic and Business Research at the University of Warwick. I am also especially grateful to Professor Cowling, Professor Pyatt, J. R. Sargent, N. Ireland and D. Heathfield for their advice and encouragement. The Engineering Industry Training Board financed most of the research contained here and my thanks go to their research staff who always proved extremely helpful. Without the efforts of Kay Herbert and Valerie Hancock the empirical results contained in this book would never have been completed. Finally, Jane Wright and Mary Crouch did a splendid job typing various drafts of this book.

# 1  Introduction, aims and scope

The aim of this study is to investigate whether there exists a realistic theory of production. One can hardly claim that economists have ignored the study of production functions. The published literature has already reached considerable proportions and is still growing rapidly. Despite the widespread interest (or perhaps because of it), the area lacks a consensus of opinion. Yet an understanding of the technology of production is crucial to the development of realistic theories and to the formulation of a wide range of policies. Of all the areas that we might distinguish, it probably has the most widespread and important implications for other economic theories.

In arriving at its present state, the economic theory of production has travelled a long and tortuous path. The bulk of empirical work still rests on functional forms which are the direct descendants of the work of Cobb and Douglas (1928). Yet at the present time there is an undercurrent of distrust of this theory. The good empirical performance of the neoclassical estimates is in stark contrast to the widely held belief that, at best, the theory is a gross simplification of the real world. This tension has been intensified by the results of work on aggregation – such as those by Fisher (1969, 1971) – which have emphasised the stringency of the conditions that must be fulfilled before rigorous aggregation is possible, and by the growth of rival theories descended from the vintage models of Johansen (1959) and and Salter (1966).

The tension that has developed has induced the protagonists in the debate to search for evidence that one or other of the alternative theories is correct. It is probably true to say that the vintage theories have not yet been properly tested. This is mainly a consequence of the empirical success of the neoclassical functions, but partly due to the demanding data requirements of the more recent theories. The inability to provide conclusive empirical evidence has led to a number of attempts to reconcile the alternative schools of thought. The most recent of these is by Johansen (1972) and is based on the thesis that different theories are relevant to different levels of aggregation and over different periods of time. Johansen's intention was to construct a number of related economic boxes into which existing theories can be meaningfully slotted, rather that to replace the existing body of knowledge. The end-product is an integrated theory of production drawing on the more important strands of the present theories. An attempt to reconcile the opposing factions seems timely given the disarray of the current theory and given the central role that production functions play in economics.

The concept of an integrated production schema appears to be an important theoretical advance, and it is adopted as a framework for organising the research undertaken here. In this way, it is possible to ask formally whether the theory adds

1

significantly to our present understanding of the production process and, in particular, whether it makes the existing theories any more tenable. Such an assessment must include a critique of the schema as a theoretical construct as well as tests of the more important concepts integrated within its framework. Although the work reports estimates of the more important production functions, particular attention is paid to vintage models, where little empirical work has so far been carried out.

A brief summary of the Johansen schema is provided in Chapter 2. It is argued that it is not an additional theory of production, but that it represents a number of related boxes into which existing (or new) theories can be placed. It is demonstrated that the schema can incorporate both the fixed-coefficient and neoclassical extremes. Consistency between these is reached by varying the level of aggregation and the time horizon. Chapter 2 also reviews some of the more important generalisations that Johansen has added to the theory. It is argued that the concept of an integrated production system is extremely flexible in the sense that it can be made relevant to a wide variety of industrial situations. However, it seems unlikely that the more sophisticated versions of the theory will be empirically testable given the crudity of the available data. The final section of Chapter 2 looks at the implications of the schema for one particular area of economics. Tracing the implications through all of the various areas would be a mammoth task, and therefore this study limits itself to considering the schema as a vehicle for reconciling the opposing factions in the manpower-planning debate (i.e. the 'manpower requirements' and the 'rate of return' schools).

After reviewing the existing theories of production one almost automatically feels a sympathy for anything as refreshing and well thought out as Johansen's work. Chapter 3, however, attempts to expose a number of important deficiencies associated with the construct and with the theories that Johansen chooses to slot into the various economic boxes. The first is the relevance of vintage theory to production in engineering and, in particular, to the nature of technical change (i.e. whether it is embodied or disembodied and whether pure vintages can be distinguished). The second section of the chapter attempts to show that the *ex ante* function requires a great deal more theoretical rigour if it is to play the central role that vintage theory accords it. A further problem with vintage theory is associated with the restrictive assumption of profit maximisation. It is demonstrated in the third section that only limited elements of the new managerial and behavioural theories can be introduced into the theoretical framework. Finally, a question mark is placed against all of the existing works that attempt to reconcile the alternative theories of production. In the case of the Johansen model, the dispute is not with the theoretical rigour of the explanation of the existence of substitution possibilities in macro functions, but with any attempt to extend this result to explain the good empirical performance of neoclassical functions found in the published literature.

The weakest link in vintage theory appears to be the *ex ante* function, and Chapter 4 explores some of the avenues that promise to make this function a much more useful concept. It is argued that an *ex ante* region is more realistic than a unique function that is technically given at each point in time. If the concept of a region is adopted, then it becomes necessary to find some means of handling movements within its boundaries if it is to play a practical role within a production schema. Here the works of Sato (1974) and Nordhaus (1969) appear to be particularly useful.

The empirical tests of the theories were based on data drawn from the UK engineering industries. The reason for this was that engineering is a key sector of the economy and probably has the most comprehensive data of all UK industries. Important data deficiencies nevertheless existed, and on a number of occasions it proved necessary to construct new data or to reformulate the functions so they could be estimated using existing data supplies. A major benefit of attempting research of this kind is the insight that it yields about data deficiencies and the ways in which they can be overcome. Data appendices are provided that indicate how some of the gaps that exist in current UK official statistics (i.e. estimates of investment and fuel consumption by minimum-list-heading industry) can be filled.

Given the availability of data and the nature of the functions themselves, cross-sectional estimates were considered to be most useful. The basic units of observation were minimum-list-heading industries (MLHs) within the UK engineering sector. This is the most detailed information one can expect from published sources: greater disaggregation would involve collecting data from individual firms, along the lines of Layard et al. (1971). Despite the level of aggregation, information was available that enabled results to be obtained for a time series of cross-sections. Nerlove (1966) and Nelson (1973) see this two-dimensional pool of information as the key to obtaining meaningful estimates of the underlying technology of production.

A variety of production functions are estimated at different levels of aggregation. Chapter 5 investigates the most detailed level, which is concerned with individual production processes such as welding and turning. Some useful links are drawn here with the work being undertaken at the Science Policy Research Unit (Sussex University), whose qualitative approach is largely consistent with the simplest Johansen schema. Relationships estimated at this level had to be estimated in employment-function (as opposed to production-function) form because of severe data constraints. The functions perform reasonably well and give important insights about the underlying *ex ante* technologies.

The success of the micro study indicated that it might be worth estimating putty-clay functions at a higher level of aggregation, where the loss in theoretical rigour appears to be offset by the existence of more complete and reliable data. Despite the wealth of employment and production function studies, remarkably little work has been carried out using vintage models. In order to provide a basis for empirical research, Chapter 6 develops a putty–clay model, consistent with the Johansen schema and the general body of vintage theory, that can be estimated on the basis of the UK data. The functions, which still distinguish particular labour skills and capital types, perform reasonably well, giving some support for the vintage approach.

The final part of the empirical work is reported in Chapter 7 and looks at the greatest level of aggregation used in this study (i.e. across MLHs for all production activities in combination). A number of production functions drawn from the constant elasticity of substitution (CES) class of technologies are estimated. The results are largely consistent with the existence of substitution possibilities according to the simplest of the CES models. An attempt is made to find if there are differences in the results between industries within engineering. In addition, 'quality' and 'performance' variables are included in the regressions, along the lines of Griliches and Ringstad (1971). Not all of these additional variables fit neatly into the neoclassical framework. Some relate to aspects of the technology that have been given scant coverage in the literature, and others relate more to market structure and industrial performance than to the technology of production. Chapter 7 demonstrates that, although aggregate neoclassical production functions appear to perform well empirically, the results give some cause for concern. Their empirical performance is much less acceptable when labour productivity appears as the dependent variable in place of output. The traditional capital and labour variables nevertheless prove to be significant explanatory variables, but the success of the 'performance' variables suggests that the explanation of labour productivity requires a more dynamic approach that does not draw only on the theory of production.

In Chapter 8, the final touches are put to the theoretical part of the study. Consideration is given to the arguments that have been put forward to explain the fundamental contradiction between functions thought to be intuitively plausible (based on vintage theory) and those that appear to arise from empirical research (based on neoclassical theory). It is argued that none of the current approaches (including Johansen's) is a complete explanation of the phenomenon. An alternative avenue is investigated that involves the construction of a 'surrogate' production function. Although the 'Cambridge controversy' has so far added little to our understanding of the empirical results, it is pointed out that certain parts of it can be salvaged to yield valuable insights about the contradiction. The explanation put forward indicates that the traditional (neoclassical) estimates are only indirectly related to the underlying technology of production.

Chapter 9 ties the remaining loose ends together and a number of conclusions are drawn. The most important of these is that only now is a realistic theory of production beginning to emerge. This new theory is much more flexible that its traditional counterparts: different technologies are associated with different production situations. The bulk of existing theory is dismissed as largely misleading as a description of the underlying technology of production. It is argued that, if we wish to say anything about the production function, data of a much more detailed kind must be used. Nevertheless, the more traditional neoclassical results do not arise by chance, but because competitive forces constrain the set of economically viable technologies to lie on a function of this type. There is no reason to suppose that

4

such models will be any the less useful for forecasting or modelling so long as the causes of the relationship are understood. This conclusion obviously is important for the theoretician, but it is also relevant for industry and government planners who have used neoclassical theory as a basis for modelling and forecasting without fully understanding the tools they have employed.

# 2  The Johansen schema

**Introduction**

The aim of this chapter is to provide an understanding of the nature and implications of the Johansen schema. It is therefore essential to grasp the concepts that are used and the ways in which they are linked with one another. The most informative way in which to introduce the concepts is with aid of a flow chart, shown here as Figure 2.1 The chart is instructive in so far as it demonstrates the links

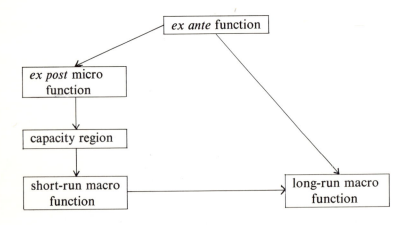

Fig. 2.1   The integrated production system

between the models and emphasises the importance of the *ex ante* function (which is a relatively neglected part of the model).

The schema is entirely consistent with and closely allied to the putty–clay theory of production proposed in the pioneering works of Salter (1966) and Johansen (1959). The *ex ante* function represents the 'putty' state, while the *ex post* micro function (in its simplest form) reflects the 'clay' aspect of the model. While the *ex post* production units can be aggregated to a form easily recognised by the vintage theorist, Johansen (1972) chooses an alternative approach to aggregation to obtain the short-run macro function.

The schema is a much more flexible description of the technology of production than are its predecessors. In distinguishing alternative levels of aggregation and time horizons, the model integrates even the extreme theories of production (i.e.

fixed-coefficient and neoclassical). In addition, the short-run macro function can itself take a variety of forms (depending on the size and distribution of established production units in the input–output space), including CES functions. It is somewhat misleading, therefore, to associate a given Johansen concept with any particular existing theory of production. It is probably more appropriate to consider the schema as a set of related economic boxes, into which alternative theories of production can be slotted. Figure 2.2 outlines the theories that Johansen has chosen to place in these boxes.

| *Johansen concept* *Existing theory* | *Ex ante* | *Ex post* micro | Feasible region | Short-run macro | Putty–clay | Long-run |
|---|---|---|---|---|---|---|
| Neoclassical | √ | | | √ | √ | √ |
| Leontief | | √ | | √ | | |
| Linear programming | | | √ | √ | √ | |

Fig. 2.2   Some links with existing theories of production

The traditional theories of production tend to take up extreme positions: at one end of the continuum there is the fixed-coefficient (or Leontief) model, which denies the possibility of substitution between the various inputs; at the other extreme is the neoclassical theory of production, where all inputs tend to be direct substitutes for one another. Figure 2.2 demonstrates that, in certain industrial situations, it is possible to conceive of a broader theory of production that is reconciliatory in the sense that it incorporates the extreme positions but relegates them to more subordinate roles. The extremes appear at opposite ends of the spectrum in terms of the level of aggregation and the time horizon.

**The Johansen concepts**

In this section, consideration is given to each of the concepts that Johansen incorporates in his integrated system of production. The most straightforward form of the schema is considered here and the generalisations that have been proposed are left until the next section. During the outline of the various concepts, an attempt is made to emphasise the links between them.

The connection between the schema and putty–clay theory has already been noted. This theory allows substitution to take place *ex ante*, i.e. before the investment decision is finalised. The *ex ante* function attempts to summarise the alternative technologies that are available to the firm when making its investment decision. Salter (1966, p. 15) has defined it as the 'production function which includes all possible designs', and as such it is 'purely technically determined' and 'free from the influence of factor prices'. The function is, in effect, the efficient envelope of all the alternative production technologies conceived of by designers and available to managers at the time when the investment decision is made.

The exact nature of the function is still in some doubt. Salter (1966) adopted the early Robinson view that substitution was relevant only in an *ex ante* sense. The Robinson (1971) view seems to have hardened, and the *ex ante* possibilities available to the firm at a given time are represented by a single point in the input–output space. Harcourt (1972, pp. 55–6) argues, however, that, although we might dismiss the *ex ante* function that spans national boundaries, we might at a national-industry level concede the existence of 'a small arc of "best-practice" possibilities'. Johansen (1972, p. 196) adopts this position and argues in favour of a unique *ex ante* function with 'classical' properties [1] at any given time.

The Johansen and Robinson views are not inconsistent. Johansen (1972, p. 9) argues that, in general, very few of the points from any particular *ex ante* function are observed, because most are associated with technologies that nobody wants and that therefore are not developed. He argues however, that all points potentially exist and could be developed given research-and-development (R & D) effort (we leave the problems of introducing R & D into the analysis until Chapter 4 below). Johansen (1972, pp. 7–8) argues that different points may be associated with different pieces of capital. If a suitable common measure of heterogeneous capital goods cannot be found, then the model collapses to the Robinson form. If such a measure can be found, the 'as if' *ex ante* function may become appropriate. For simplicity of exposition, in this section all factors of production are assumed to be current inputs. Johansen's treatment of capital is discussed in greater detail in Chapter 3. The assumption of a unique *ex ante* function with 'classical' properties is obviously a gross simplification.

Figure 2.3 illustrates the *ex ante* function at various points in time. For simplicity, only the isoquants associated with the optimal scale of output, $Y^*$, are shown in the input per unit of output space at various points in time, $t, t+1, t+2, \ldots$. The points $A, B, C \ldots$ describe the input–output coefficients of technologies actually drawn from the *ex ante* space and hence observed. The figure shows just two axes from what may, in practice, be a multidimensional space. We may write the equation

$$Y_t = f_t(Q_t^1, Q_t^2) \tag{2.1}$$

for the two-input case, where $f(\ )$ has 'classical' properties. [2] Normally the variables drawn from the *ex ante* function will be associated with full capacity working $\tilde{Y}_t = f_t(\tilde{Q}_t^1, \tilde{Q}_t^2)$, where $\sim$ denotes full capacity and $Q$ is a current output.

8

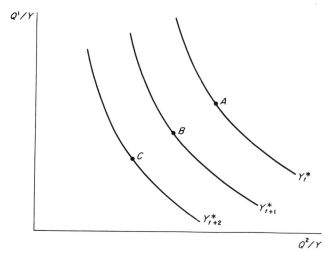

Fig. 2.3   The *ex ante* function at various points in time

### *The* ex post *micro function*

The *ex post* micro function becomes relevant once the investment decision has been finalised. It is derived directly from the *ex ante* function given prevailing (or expected) factor prices. Figure 2.4 shows the case of firm $F_A$, faced by factor prices $(q^1, q^2)$ and wishing to establish production facilities at the optimal scale of output, $Y_t^*$. Its cost-minimising choice of technology is $(Q_t^{1*}, Q_t^{2*})$, where one of the isocost lines ($C^* = r_t Q_t + w_t Q_t$) is tangent to $Y_t^* = f_t(Q^1, Q^2)$. Once $F_A$ has established the new production unit, the production function collapses to a single point, $A$, and the associated isoquant is denoted $\tilde{Y}_{At}$. Figure 2.4 is analogous to that used by Svennilson (1964, p. 111).

The most promising way of defining the relationship in the Johansen world is for a given vintage of capital used in a given process in a known firm:

$$Y_{jxv} = \frac{1}{\zeta_{jxv}^1} Q_{jxv}^1 = \frac{1}{\zeta_{jxv}^2} Q_{jxv}^2 \tag{2.2}$$

where all of the variables and parameters are of the same time period. The variables $Y$, $Q^1$ and $Q^2$ take values such that $0 \leq Y \leq \tilde{Y}, 0 \leq Q^1 \leq \tilde{Q}^1$ and $0 \leq Q^2 \leq \tilde{Q}^2$; $\xi^1$ and $\xi^2$ are constants. The subscripts $j, x, v$ denote the $j$th firm ($j = 1, \ldots, m$), the $x$th production process ($x = 1, \ldots, s$), and the $v$th vintage of capital ($v = 1, \ldots, T$ – where $T$ denotes the oldest vintage still in use). The new production regime corresponds to the traditional Leontief form. While the translation from a function exhibiting substitution possibilities to one with technical rigidity is the key feature of putty–clay models, what distinguishes the Johansen (1972) approach from the bulk of vintage growth theory is the level of aggregation at which the relationship is

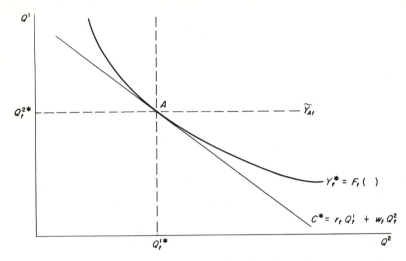

Fig. 2.4 Derivation of the *ex post* micro function from the *ex ante* alternatives

expected to hold. Johansen argues that it most realistic to assume that the relationship characterises a production unit, where this may be a single piece of equipment or possibly a section of a plant.

The form of equation (2.2) implies that there are constant returns to scale in the use of production units. The more general case, where $\xi^1 = \xi^1(\tilde{Q}^1 - Q^1)$ and $\xi^2 = \xi^2(\tilde{Q}^2 - Q^2)$ is considered by Johansen (1972, pp. 46–50) and in the next section of this chapter. No time subscripts have been added to the variables or coefficients, but in the real world disembodied technical change will affect $\xi^1$ and $\xi^2$, while physical decay or learning may affect $Q^1$ and $Q^2$. Although a number of studies have looked at the adjustment of input–output coefficients, their work has tended to be very aggregate. [3]

*The capacity region*

Johansen attempts to develop a theory that adequately describes the micro situation. The micro 'building blocks' are used as the basis for constructing more aggregate models. Approaching the problem in this way enables the researcher to 'stop off' at any particular level of aggregation (whether it is at the level of a section of a plant, a plant, a firm or an industry). It is to the problem of aggregating individual production units that we now turn. Given that the underlying micro technologies are adequately summarised by equation (2.2), if we overlook the existence of different sections of a firm, then the capacity (or feasible) region can be represented by the space defined by the following constraints:

10

$$\sum_j \sum_v \xi^i_{jv} Y_{jv} \leq S^i \tag{2.3}$$

$$Y_{jv} \leq \tilde{Y}_{jv} \tag{2.4}$$

$$0 \leq Y_{jv}, 0 \leq S^i \tag{2.5}$$

where $i$ denotes the $i$th input ($i = 1, 2, \ldots$); $\xi^i_{jv}$ refers to the input of the $i$th factor per unit of output used by the $v$th vintage of the $j$th firm; and $S^i$ denotes the supply of the $i$th input to the industry.

The first inequality, (2.3), defines the set of available production units that can be utilised given sufficiently large supplies of the factors of production. Each production unit is defined by inequality (2.4) to operate in the region at or below full capacity. Finally, inequality (2.5) states that only positive levels of inputs and outputs are relevant.

In order to carry out the theoretical analysis expediently, Johansen chooses to work in continuous terms. In order to do this he defines the capacity distribution,

$$f(\xi^1, \xi^2) \Delta \xi^1 \Delta \xi^2 \tag{2.6}$$

which is the output potential of production units the technology coefficients of which fall in the region $\xi^1$ to $\xi^1 + \Delta \xi^1$ and $\xi^2$ to $\xi^2 + \Delta \xi^2$. This continuous analogue to the linear programming case has its capacity region wherever $f(\ ) > 0$. (Subscripts – $j, x, v$ – can be added to the coefficients as required.)

*The short-run macro function*

The imposition of some form of managerial behaviour (for instance, output maximisation) on the linear framework of the capacity region enables a list of preferences about the order in which production units are utilised to be derived. In linear programming form, the production problem can be written: maximise $Y = \sum_j \sum_v Y_{jv}$, subject to equations (2.3)–(2.5) inclusive. We can write out the linear programming problem and its dual in the two-factor $m + T$ production unit case as follows.

*Linear programme*            DUAL VARIABLES

Maximise $\quad Y = \sum_{j=1}^{m} \sum_{v=1}^{T} Y_{jv}$

subject to $\quad \xi^1_1 Y_1 + \ldots \xi^1_{m+T} Y_{m+T} \leq S^1 \qquad\qquad q^1$

$\qquad\qquad \xi^2 Y_1 + \ldots \xi^2_{m+T} Y_{m+T} \leq S^2 \qquad\qquad q^2$

$\qquad\qquad Y_1 \qquad\qquad\qquad\quad \leq \tilde{Y}_1 \qquad\qquad z_1$

$\qquad\qquad\quad Y_2 \qquad\qquad\qquad \leq \tilde{Y}_2 \qquad\qquad z_2$

$\qquad\qquad\qquad\qquad\quad Y_{m+T} \leq \tilde{Y}_{m+T} \qquad\quad z_{m+T} \tag{2.7}$

$Y_1 \geq 0, \ldots, Y_{m+T} \geq 0; S^1 \geq 0; S^2 \geq 0$

11

*Dual problem*

Minimise $\quad q^1 S^1 + q^2 S^2 + \sum_{j=1}^{m} \sum_{v=1}^{T} z_{jv} Y_{jv}$

subject to $\quad q^1 \xi_1^1 + q^2 \xi_1^2 + z_1 \geq 1$

$$q^1 \xi_{m+T}^1 + q^2 \xi_{m+T}^2 + z_{m+T} \geq 1$$

$$\xi_1^1 \geq 0, \ldots, \xi_{m+T}^1 \geq 0; \xi_1^2 \geq 0, \ldots, \xi_{m+T}^2 \geq 0 \qquad (2.8)$$

The dual is obtained by transposing the coefficient matrix in (2.7) and using the coefficients 1 of the objective function ($Y = \sum_j \sum_v Y_{jv}$) as constants in the right-hand side of the inequalities in (2.8).

The values $q^1$ and $q^2$ can be interpreted as shadow prices of the inputs in terms of units of output. Whether a production unit is operated or not depends on the value of $q_{jv}^1 \xi_{jv}^1 + q_{jv}^2 \xi_{jv}^2$. Where this value exceeds unity ($z_{jv} < 0$), the unit is laid up; and where it is less than unity ($z_{jv} > 0$), it is operated. We interpret $z_{jv}$ as the quasi-rent of the $v$th vintage of the $j$th firm.

Summation of output and inputs over production units that earn non-negative quasi-rents yields the aggregate variables $Y$, $Q^1$ and $Q^2$. The short-run production function at the macro level is defined by

$$Y = F(Q^1, Q^2) \qquad (2.9)$$

Johansen (1972, pp. 37–40) again finds it useful to translate this function into continuous terms. In order to do this, he defines the set of points $(\xi^1, \xi^2)$ that earn a non-negative quasi-rent as

$$G(q^1, q^2) = \{(\xi^1, \xi^2) \mid \xi^1 > 0, \xi^2 > 0, q^1 \xi^1 + q^2 \xi^2 < 1\} \qquad (2.10)$$

The capacity distribution for a small cell was summarised by equation (2.6). Integration over all such cells, where there are production units that earn non-negative quasi-rents, yields the aggregate variables

$$Y = \iint_{G(\quad)} f(\quad) d\xi^1 d\xi^2 \qquad (2.11)$$

$$Q^i = \iint_{G(\quad)} \xi^i f(\quad) d\xi^1 d\xi^2 \qquad (2.12)$$

which enter equation (2.9), the short-run macro function.

Johansen (1972, pp. 55–62), with full mathematical rigour, demonstrates that the marginal products of the macro function are

$$\partial Y/\partial Q^1 = q^1 \quad \text{and} \quad \partial Y/\partial Q^2 = q^2 \qquad (2.13)$$

and that the slope of the isoquant is given by

$$\left. \frac{dQ^2}{dQ^1} \right|_{dY=0} = -\frac{q^1}{q^2} \qquad (2.14)$$

Returns to scale (ibid., pp. 64–7), $e$, depend on the distribution of capacity in the input per unit of output space, but $e < 1$ in all cases. The elasticity of substitution between factors, $\sigma$ (ibid., pp. 67–72), depends on the variety of technologies at the margin; the absolute level of operations; and the amount of production capacity located in a small strip close to the zero quasi-rent line. A wide range of elasticities can be incorporated, including CES functions. Johansen (1972, pp. 81–5), for example, demonstrates that, given appropriate assumptions, a Cobb–Douglas function can be obtained.

*The putty–clay function*

Although Johansen does not discuss a putty–clay formulation in the context of the simplest schema, the functions outlined above form the basis of a putty–clay equation

$$Y^* = \sum_j \sum_v \frac{1}{\xi_{jv}^1} U_{jv} Q_{jv}^1 = \sum_j \sum_v \frac{1}{\xi_{jv}^2} U_{jv} Q_{jv}^2 \qquad (2.15)$$

In this simple case, each production unit is assumed to exhibit constant returns to scale. $U$ denotes the degree to which capacity is utilised, and we might expect, in the simple case,

$$U = \begin{cases} 0 - ve \text{ quasi-rent} \\ 1 + ve \text{ quasi-rent} \end{cases}$$

where the number of units with zero quasi-rents are assumed to be negligible.

Super-imposed on this static model is the tendency for the system to modify itself over time – in particular, by scrapping obsolete technologies and by introducing new technologies chosen from the *ex ante* function. Empirically testable putty–clay models based on this sort of approach are outlined in Chapters 5 and 6.

*The long-run macro function*

The long-run macro function described by Johansen (1972, pp. 19–25) is a highly theoretical construct. It appears to correspond to the perfectly efficient production technology (which fully utilises available supplies of resources) towards which traditional (average) functions are assumed to move. In a sector where the *ex ante* technology is continually improving and/or factor supplies are changing over time, the long-run macro function is unlikely to be static. Hence, the average production function is unlikely to catch it up. The function is constructed on the basis of factor supplies, $S^i$, available to the sector at a particular time. It is assumed, however, that the stock of capital available can take any form desired. The form chosen is that that maximises the output of the sector for the existing factor ratio, and it is fairly obvious that this information will be isolated from the most up-to-date *ex ante* function.

Consider an *ex ante* function that exhibits first increasing, and then decreasing, returns to scale. In this case there will exist an optimal size of production unit the factor inputs of which will be drawn from the optimal *ex ante* function associated with this factor ratio. We can write

$$\tilde{Q}^i = \tilde{Q}^i(S^1, S^2, \ldots, S^n) = \tilde{Q}^i(\ ) \tag{2.16}$$

for the *i*th factor, $i = 1, 2, \ldots, n$; where $Q^i$ and $S^i$ denote, respectively, the demand for and supply of the *i*th factor. The values, $Q^i$, must obviously satisfy the *ex ante* function

$$Y^* = f[\tilde{Q}^1(\ ), \tilde{Q}^2(\ ), \ldots, \tilde{Q}^n(\ )] = f[\ ] \tag{2.17}$$

Writing the input–output coefficients,

$$\xi^1 = \frac{Q^1(\ )}{f[\ ]}, \ldots, \xi^n = \frac{Q^n(\ )}{f[\ ]} \tag{2.18}$$

we have *n* equations in *n* unknowns (i.e. $\xi^1, \ldots, \xi^n$), and hence we can isolate the 'technique relation',

$$g(\xi^1, \xi^2, \ldots, \xi^n) = 1 \tag{2.19}$$

which is the unit isoquant of the long-run macro function. In addition, however, because all firms are the same size and have the same input ratio, it follows that

$$\xi^i = S^i/Y \tag{2.20}$$

where $Y$ is the industry output from all production units established. Thus, we can write the more general form of the 'technique relation',

$$g^*\left(\frac{S^1}{Y}, \ldots, \frac{S^n}{Y}\right) = 1$$

with the implied production function,

$$g^*(S^1, \ldots, S^n) = Y \tag{2.21}$$

exhibiting constant returns to scale.

The unit isoquant of the short-run macro function corresponding to each level of output coincides in a unique curve in the input–output space. Those of an *ex ante* function exhibiting first increasing and then decreasing returns to scale form a family of curves to the north-east of the isoquant associated with the optimal scale of output. Only the most efficient *ex ante* unit isoquant and the technique relationship coincide. It is fairly obvious that the family of *ex ante* isoquants will generally fail to correspond with those of the long-run macro function except at the optimal level of output of the *ex ante* function. Where the *ex ante* function exhibits constant returns to scale, the isoquants of the two functions at any given level of output will coincide. In the case where the *ex ante* function is homothetic, the isoquant maps will look alike but isoquants that coincide will be associated with different levels of output, except at the optimal *ex ante* output level. The maps will look entirely different in the case of the non-homothetic *ex ante* function, except at the optimal level.

14

## Generalisations to the schema

Johansen has made a number of suggestions about the ways in which the schema can be generalised. It is unnecessary to document all of these, and this section merely records some of the more interesting changes.

### The ex ante *function*

Johansen (1972, p. 7) has argued that it may be necessary (particularly when undertaking empirical work) to distinguish shift-working or overtime working in the *ex ante* function. The simplest generalisation is the case of a shift-system characterised by two identical shifts:

$$Y = 2f(K, L) \tag{2.22}$$

A report by the National Board for Prices and Incomes (1970, pp. 1–3) suggests the existence of a diversity of shift systems in the UK, and empirical evidence in the *Ministry of Labour Gazette* (1954, 1965) indicates that different systems operate alongside one another even in the same industry. As regards the toolmaking industry, for instance, Senker et al. (1975, p. 74) note that there is a tendency, where sophisticated equipment is worked on a multiple-shift system, for traditional capital to be employed only on the main shift. Equation (2.22) is therefore an oversimplification, but in principle there is no reason why the *ex ante* function should not be appropriately generalised. It should be noted, however, that the cost function will also be more complicated.

Johansen (1972, p. 8) argues that it may prove difficult to justify a single *ex ante* function that summarises the technical knowledge (at the intensive margin) that is available to everyone everywhere without cost. While normative theory will be interested in the efficient (boundary) *ex ante* function constructed from all of the functions perceived by potential investors, a positive theory would require each function seen by the investors to be separately distinguished. Johansen (1972, p. 9) also realised that it was extremely unlikely that all of the technologies from a particular *ex ante* function would be needed. If they are not, it is unlikely that they would be developed and thereby observed. Johansen argues that such points potentially exist and would appear as the result of R & D effort, but he seems uncertain about how this new dimension can be introduced into the theory. This problem is reviewed in Chapter 4, and the works of Nordhaus (1974) and Sato (1974) are used to provide an answer.

In an earlier article, Johansen (1959, pp. 160–1 and 166) suggested that established capacity might be included as an argument in the *ex ante* function. This variable would be related to the pressure on natural resources or the availability of external economies or diseconomies (see Johansen, 1972, p. 6). More generally still, the form of the *ex ante* function might change with the size of established capacity.

### Ex post *micro functions*

Despite the assumption of technical rigidity, Johansen (1972, pp. 10–13) considers it likely that there will be 'some scope' for *ex post* substitution at the micro level. Vintage models have been developed that allow *ex post* substitution. Solow (1960) and Phelps (1962), for example, developed putty–putty models where the *ex post* substitution conformed with the *ex ante* technology except that capital was assumed given at its end of the period value (modified only by disembodied changes and deterioration). Park (1966) follows this approach, but allows *ex post* substitution according to a more or less restricted part of the *ex ante* isoquant map. Johansen (1972, p. 11) introduces the notation necessary to deal with even more general cases, but does not use it in his analysis. He claims (ibid., p. 13) that the simple formulation can, with some reservations, be treated as a good approximation to reality in many cases.

These reservations are linked with the important generalisations that Johansen (1972, pp. 46–53) introduces. The method of dealing with shift-working and over-time in the *ex ante* function, for example, is carried over directly to the *ex post* micro technologies. Each shift is allowed to have its own $\xi^1$, $\xi^2$ points; similarly, normal hours may have one $\xi^1$, $\xi^2$ combination, while overtime hours have another. A further generalisation allows the input–output coefficients to vary as output varies in the range

$$0 < Y < \tilde{Y}$$

according to

$$
\begin{array}{lll}
Q^1 = Q^1(Y) & dQ^1/dY > 0 & d^2(Q^1)/dY^2 \gtreqless 0 \\
Q^2 = Q^2(Y) & dQ^2/dY > 0 & d^2(Q^2)/dY^2 \gtreqless 0
\end{array}
\tag{2.23}
$$

The constant returns-to-scale property ensured the existence of a single point in the input–output space, but now the capacity distribution appears along a given curve, defined by equations (2.23) and written

$$\xi^1 = h(\xi^2) \tag{2.24}$$

where $h$ is an increasing function. In practice, this makes no difference to the theoretical analysis, as marginal production units are utilised up to the point where the marginal costs of production (valued on the basis of shadow prices) are equal to each other and to unity, providing, of course, that the expansion curves intersect the zero quasi-rent line. The capacity of production units in the space $\xi^1$ to $\xi^1 + \Delta\xi^1$ and $\xi^2$ to $\xi^2 + \Delta\xi^2$ can still be represented by $f(\xi^1, \xi^2)\Delta\xi^1\Delta\xi^2$ for a small cell, and the theoretical analysis outlined by Johansen (1972, sections 31–4) still applies. Johansen adds, however, that for empirical analysis this generalisation complicates matters considerably.

Where marginal input requirements are decreasing over the whole range of output levels up to $\tilde{Y}_j$, production units will either be fully utilised or not utilised at all. Production units are now represented in the calculations by their input requirements at full-capacity utilisation $(\xi^1, \xi^2)$. Where marginal input requirements are first decreasing and then increasing as $Y \to \tilde{Y}$, we know that no production units in the range $0 < Y_j < Y_j^*$ will be employed, where $Y^*$ denotes the level of output associated with the minimum input requirements per unit of output. Production

16

units can then be represented by increasing curves such as equation (2.28) – and such units will be employed at a level of output $Y_j$, such that $Y_j^* < Y_j < \tilde{Y}_j$, where their marginal costs are again equal to each other and equal to unity. It should again be possible to summarise established capacity in a small cell by $f(\xi^1, \xi^2)$ $\Delta\xi^1\Delta\xi^2$ and the theory remains the same.

*Short-run macro function*

The final generalisation concerns the efficiency assumption that underlies the short-run macro function. A positive theory where the short-run macro function is based on less-than-perfect efficiency is likely to be more realistic. If we write this function as

$$Y = \iint Uf(\ )d\xi^1 d\xi^2$$

$$Q^i = \iint \xi^i Uf(\ )d\xi^1 d\xi^2 \qquad (2.25)$$

and rewrite the quasi-rent line as

$$z = \frac{p - q^1\xi^1 - q^2\xi^2}{p} = 1 - \frac{q^1}{p}\xi^1 - \frac{q^2}{p}\xi^2 \qquad (2.26)$$

where $p$ denotes final output prices, then, for perfect optimisation,

$$U(z) = \begin{cases} 0 & \text{when } z \leq 0 \\ 1 & \text{when } z \geq 0 \end{cases} \qquad (2.27)$$

where $U$ denotes the degree to which productive capacity and inputs are utilised.
Johansen (1972, pp. 50–3) considers the more general case where $U(z)$ is a non-decreasing function, such that $0 \leq U(z) \leq 1$. The short-run macro function is now written not as $F(Q^1, Q^2)$ but as $F(Q^1, Q^2, U)$, where

$$F(Q^1, Q^2, U) < F(Q^1, Q^2)$$

except where $U$ has the perfect optimisation form. Even more general forms of $U$ can be envisaged; for example,

$$U = U\left(z, \frac{Y}{\tilde{Y}}\right)$$

where profitability considerations are, to some extent, pushed into the background. (One example might be where there are consumer–buyer links not wholly dependent on prices.)

**The implications of the schema for the manpower planning debate [4]**

The central role that the theory of production plays in economics derives mainly from the large number of areas that it permeates: growth theory, welfare economics, manpower planning and the theory of the trade cycle all to a great extent rely on the characteristics of the underlying technology of production. Equilibrium in the labour market, for example, is the result of balancing the demands for various skills with the corresponding supplies, where the demand relationships are based on the production function (which defines the possibilities of substitution between capital types and labour skills).

This section attempts to illustrate the importance of a sound knowledge of the production process when assessing the role to be played by manpower planning in establishing equilibrium in the labour market. Evidence about the ease of substitution between factors would be invaluable in resolving the debate about how much and what type of manpower planning should be undertaken. Little further has been said since Blaug's authoritative work (1970), and yet the theory of production has been developing in a way that has important implications for manpower planning.

If any conclusion at all can be drawn from the preceding sections, it is that ideally we require a theory of production that is able to encompass all of the alternative situations: short-run and long-run, macro and micro. This is the direction in which economic theory has been moving, and Johansen's schema can be seen as the end-product of this trend. The schema reconciles the extreme theories of production by making different functional forms relevant to different production situations. It is this aspect of the Johansen model that could prove valuable in delimiting the areas where the 'manpower-forecasting' and 'rate-of-return' analyses should be used, and in providing insights about how the two approaches may be combined. Ahamad and Blaug (1973, pp. 322–3) argue that manpower planning should develop by combining the two approaches.

### The manpower-requirements/rate-of-return debate

The integrated production schema assumes that substitution is possible between different factors of production in the long run, and that if factor prices are flexible they are able to play an allocative role. Under these conditions, neoclassical production functions can be used to yield estimates of marginal products for use in rate-of-return calculations. In deciding about optimal educational strategies, the conditions will be ideal for 'rate-of-return' analysis. In other words, it should be possible to make broad comparisons between the benefits of extra education or training (for instance, the cumulative discounted value of marginal products or wages) and its costs.

In the short run, however, the production system indicates a world that is much less flexible and that corresponds broadly to a fixed-coefficient technology. In a world where substitution between skills is more limited, comparisons of the sort outlined above are no longer a sound basis for making decisions about the amount or nature of training. It would appear that the appropriate approach in this case would be to predict the magnitude of employment-by-skill that is just sufficient to produce the desired level of output, and then, for members of each skill category, rate-of-return comparisons can be made. These should enable the optimal level and type of training to be found for each group. As the factor-requirement calculations are based on a linear programming analysis, shadow prices for each type of input can be estimated directly and (as these are analogous to the marginal products of neo-classical theory – see Baumol and Quandt, 1963) can be used in the rate-of-return calculations.

The use of linear programming analysis in the short run enables labour-market rigidities to be built into the model. Where it is considered to be useful, the solution to the linear programming problem can be made contingent upon given factor supplies. As the planning horizon lengthens, we expect the rigid labour-supply functions to give way to more elastic functions. So far, however, the traditional neoclassical employment models have not been introduced into simultaneous systems alongside labour-supply functions.

The use of an integrated production system could help avoid many of the criticisms that have been aimed at the manpower-forecasting approach. First, it avoids assuming the existence of an unchanging relationship between inputs, which in the past has been the hallmark of the manpower-requirements approach. Second, although the schema is demand-oriented, its links with linear program-ming analysis allow supply features (via the constraints) to play some role. Third, using the simulation capabilities of the linear programming approach, it should be possible to make short- and medium-term, multivalued forecasts (contingent on output growth, investment behaviour and factor supplies). This should avoid the important criticism of past forecasts made by Blaug (1970, pp. 159–66), that they could not be evaluated because they were single-valued predictions based on assumptions that, in retrospect, proved to be false. Fourth, the relative prices of inputs (as in all putty–clay models) play a key part in determining (a) the character-istics of new technologies chosen and (b) which of the existing technologies are utilised. Finally, despite the demand-oriented approach that the schema implies for the short to medium run, rate-of-return analysis can still be used to yield a picture of optimal short-run training strategies for particular skills. Having already predicted the absolute levels of demand for these skills using a manpower requirements approach, the costs and benefits of various training strategies can be compared using rate-of-return analysis. This is a step in the direction of integrating the two approaches, which Ahamad and Blaug (1973, pp. 319–20) deem to be desirable.

*The company–industry planning debate*

One final way in which the Johansen schema may contribute to reconciling various factions in the manpower-planning arena is by removing any conflict between firm- and industry-level planning. The means of reconciliation is through the integration of functions that are relevant at different levels of aggregation.

Johansen (1972, p. 4) feels that the company planner is likely immediately to recognise the relevance of the micro theory, which forms the foundation on which the more aggregate models are constructed, and thereby gain an appreciation of the macro models. In turn, any attempt by the industry planner to construct realistic

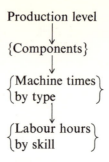

Production level
↓
{Components}
↓
⎧Machine times⎫
⎩by type          ⎭
↓
⎧Labour hours⎫
⎩by skill          ⎭

Fig. 2.5   Desired production and factor demands

macro models will induce an interest both in factors that are highly relevant at the company level and in the problems of aggregation. The gap between the industry and company planner may be partly (if not wholly) eliminated by the adoption of an integrated system of production.

The Johansen micro theory may well be valid for a variety of industries at the plant or company level. The micro theory is concerned with the short-run problem of translating a desired level of production into a consistent set of factor demands. Figure 2.5 shows the simplest sequence of events. Here, the level of output is assumed to be given and this level is translated into desired levels of output of each component part. In this simple illustration, each component can be produced only in one way and this defines the set of machine times (by type) and labour hours (by skill). Figure 2.6 however, reports a slightly more general model. The level of production again defines the desired level of output of components, but the various parts can now be produced by alternative means (for instance, a hole may be

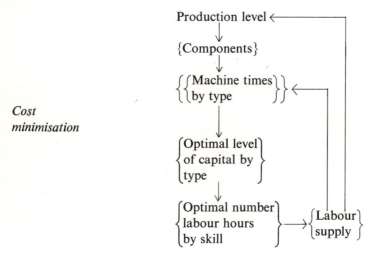

Fig. 2.6   Desired production and factor demands: a more complex view

broached rather than bored; a part may be cast rather than fabricated), and in this way a limited element of substitution is introduced. The optimal sets of labour and capital hours are chosen by cost minimisation, although (through the linear programming formulation) the choice is limited to sets consistent with the supply constraints. Alternative responses to supply conditions can be incorporated into the schema: for example, the entrepreneur may revise the desired level of output of the final product or attempt to expand recruitment or training. It is this sort of model that underlies the work on employment carried out by Bell (1972) and Senker and Huggett (1973).

The short-run micro theory is largely consistent with this sort of decision and revision process. The production manager, in particular, should be fairly happy with the Johansen picture, although he may to some extent debate the cost-minimising hypothesis and replace it by 'satisficing' behaviour. The personnel and general managers may find the model outlined above very limited, because manpower plans are only a part of the overall corporate strategy and the schema in its current form is relevant to only a part of the manpower-planning problem. In the taxonomy outlined by Chadwick (1969, p. 51) it is most relevant to the first phase: the 'overall planning' of total numbers, skill groups, organisational groups, costs, and so on. 'Individual planning' is not a central concern and little has been said about career planning, management succession, recruitment or training. However, the organisation of data for the schema would put human accounting on a formal basis and many of these interesting questions could be analysed.

Despite the recent dominance of the neoclassical theory of production and the rise of the 'rate-of-return' approach, new developments in the theory of production suggest that the 'manpower-requirements' approach still has an important role to play. The Johansen schema can be viewed as an important advance in the theory of production. Empirical work based on the Johansen model should provide the information necessary to delimit the situations in which each of these approaches is appropriate. It should be remembered, however, that manpower planning is only one of a number of possible weapons. Any decision to make use of it will depend not only on its potential benefits exceeding its costs, but also on its efficiency relative to other weapons. As for the other weapons, the current and future role of technical change should perhaps be of at least equal interest to planners. There is, of course, no reason why the schema should not be modified so that it can be used to investigate the implications of technical change for manpower requirements, or the technical changes required to balance movements in manpower supplies.


**Notes**

[1] Johansen (1972, p. 6) states that the functions have 'such properties as are usually attributed to traditional production functions'. Allen (1968, p. 44) describes these properties in some detail and they are reviewed here after the necessary notation has been introduced.

[2] Very briefly, this implies that $\partial f/\partial Q^1 > 0$ and $\partial f/\partial Q^2 > 0$ while $\partial^2 f/\partial(Q^1)^2 < 0$ and $\partial^2 f/\partial(Q^2)^2 < 0$. In addition, $Y \to \tilde{Y}^1$ and $Y \to \tilde{Y}^2$ as $\partial f/\partial Q^1 \to 0$ and $\partial f/\partial Q^2 \to 0$ respectively, where $\tilde{Y}^1$ and $\tilde{Y}^2$ denote asymptotic values of output.

[3] See for example Phillips (1955), Ghosh (1960), Stone (1963), Sevaldson (1963) and Wigley (1970). These and a number of other authors' works are reviewed by Bosworth and Evans (1973).

[4] A more detailed discussion of the link between the technology of production and manpower planning is given in Bosworth (1974a, 1975).

# 3 An integrated system of production: comments and criticisms

## Introduction

Several aspects of the schema can be criticised and most of these criticisms apply also to the more general body of vintage theory. The list of topics covered in this chapter is not exhaustive, but a number of important questions are raised. Discussion of the *ex ante* function, however, is left till the next chapter, the whole of which is devoted to this key link in putty–clay theory.

One potentially important deficiency of both the theoretical and empirical research to date concerns the treatment of *ex post* modifications to the capital stock, i.e. alterations made to machines already established and in use. What little information exists about modifications is reviewed in the next section. The traditional putty–clay and putty–putty models fail to deal adequately with this aspect of technical change and it presents some problems for the Johansen schema. In addition, some comments are made about the purchase of machines not of the latest vintage, and the suggestion that the vintage effect is not an empirically significant factor in technical change is investigated. A brief review is given of the evidence, which draws on direct observation of technologies introduced at the intensive margin, and on the empirical performance of 'average' production functions. The body of evidence associated with traditional neoclassical production functions is dismissed as largely misleading and it is argued that the Johansen schema does not provide an explanation of the empirical success of such functions. The last section of this chapter looks at the need to expand the schema beyond the restrictive assumptions of profit maximisation and perfect competition.

## The embodiment hypothesis

The idea that technical characteristics are embodied both in inputs and in outputs is fairly widely accepted and has formed the basis from which the vintage theory of production and the work on hedonic indices have been developed. While the work on embodiment has not concentrated on the capital input to the exclusion of all other inputs, capital is nevertheless a prime example of a bundle of technical characteristics (where different types of capital are represented by broadly different bundles). The concept of skills in the theory of human capital is based on a similar hypothesis, but the analogy should not be taken too far (see Blaug, 1970, pp. 1–8). Capital, more than any other input, is open to the assumption that the technical characteristics become fixed once they are embodied, and it is for this reason that vintage theory has tended to concentrate on capital rather than labour (whose skills may be altered by learning-by-doing or by more formal training).

*Modification and technical change*

The fact that capital may be modified (with some investment) has largely been overlooked in the vintage approach, particularly in empirical research. Svennilson (1964, p. 100) notes that 'The "fixation" of the technological characteristics is in fact not absolute. Machinery may to some extent be modified and improved in order to increase its efficiency. . . . Besides, equipment may be rebuilt and combined with new parts [and] such "modernisation" will require new investment. . . .' Johansen (1972, pp. 4–5) recognises modifications as a possible stumbling block that may render parts of the study irrelevant. His fear was that 'certain basic structures already acquired may facilitate the installment of new pieces of equipment, or that modernisation or reconstruction of old equipment may be more profitable than either operating the equipment in its old shape or acquiring new equipment. We would then get equipment of mixed vintages which are different from equipment of any well defined vintage, and it may be necessary to trace the whole history of individual pieces of equipment.' Even if such forms of technical change are empirically important, however, the static aspects of the integrated production schema will remain valid, and only the dynamic aspects will need modifying.

The importance of this form of technical change probably differs considerably between firms, although Svennilson (1964, p. 110) states that 'Detailed industry studies of the machinery equipment of the engineering industry carried out at the Swedish Institute of Industrial Research [Wallander, 1962] indicate that the reconditioning and rebuilding of equipment play an important part.' Examples of particular modifications can be found. Some existing types of machines have been modified to incorporate numerical-control facilities, but, because numerical control demands technical standards that are generally lacking in the original machines, this is far from commonplace. Senker et al. (1975, p. 51) found evidence that digital readouts had been added to machines already installed for use in toolmaking activities. In addition, there is some evidence of refurbishing of grinding machines where the old hydraulic systems have been replaced by electric feeds.

There is an urgent need for research into the empirical importance of modifications to capital equipment. There is little UK published information relating to this question. The data reported below are drawn from the *Census of Production* (sales of principal products) and *Business Monitor*. Tables 3.1 and 3.2 report the available data for the sales of parts, relative to total sales of complete metal cutting and metal forming machines. Both series include an element of exports and no

Table 3.1

*Census of Production*: sales of parts (£ thousand)

| Year | 1 Sales of metal cutting parts | 2 Sales of complete metal cutting machines | 3 Ratio of columns 1 to 2 (per cent) | 4 Sales of metal forming parts | 5 Sales of complete metal forming machines | 6 Ratio of columns 4 to 5 (per cent) | 7 Sales of all metal cutting and forming parts | 8 Sales of complete metal cutting and forming machines | 9 Ratio of columns 7 to 8 (per cent) |
|---|---|---|---|---|---|---|---|---|---|
| 1948[a] | 2,317 | 23,751 | 8·88 | 901 | 4,050 | 22·40 | 3,875 | 32,198 | 12·03 |
| 1951[a] | 3,607 | 34,788 | 9·39 | 1,445 | 8,431 | 17·13 | 5,885 | 45,576 | 12·91 |
| 1954[a] | 5,163 | 47,722 | 9·76 | 1,766 | 10,531 | 16.76 | 8,108 | 62,804 | 12·91 |
| 1963 | — | — | — | — | — | — | 14,530 | 108,757 | 13·36 |
| 1968 | 15,775 | 117,119 | 11·87 | 4,473 | 31,225 | 14·36 | 20,248 | 148,344 | 13·64 |

[a] The columns associated with metal cutting and metal forming machines exclude those machines which cannot easily be allocated to the appropriate heading.

Table 3.2

*Business Monitor*: expenditure on parts (£ thousand)

| Year | 1 Metal-cutting parts | 2 Metal-cutting machines | 3 Ratio 1 to 2 (per cent) | 4 Metal-forming parts | 5 Metal-forming machines | 6 Ratio 4 to 5 (per cent) | 7 All parts | 8 All machines | 9 Ratio 7 to 8 (per cent) |
|---|---|---|---|---|---|---|---|---|---|
| 1967 | 5,408 | 115,075 | 4·69 | 1,226 | 33,877 | 3·61 | 6,634 | 148,952 | 4·45 |
| 1968 | 6,083 | 114,034 | 5·33 | 1,880 | 31,120 | 6·04 | 7,963 | 145,154 | 5·48 |
| 1969 | 7,792 | 126,443 | 6·16 | 2,046 | 35,626 | 5·74 | 9,838 | 162,069 | 6·04 |
| 1970 | 9,767 | 147,971 | 6·60 | 2,709 | 38,237 | 7·08 | 12,476 | 186,208 | 6·70 |
| 1971 | 9,404 | 132,271 | 7·10 | 3,465 | 43,895 | 7·89 | 12,869 | 176,166 | 7·30 |
| 1972[a] | 17,118 | 106,460 | 16·07 | 6,704 | 43,196 | 15·51 | 23,822 | 149,656 | 15·91 |
| 1973 | 20,439 | 120,551 | 16·95 | 8,825 | 49,744 | 17·74 | 29,264 | 170,295 | 17·18 |
| 1974[b] | 12,562 | 60,742 | 20·68 | 4,332 | 26,655 | 16·25 | 16,894 | 87,397 | 19·33 |

[a] Series not compatible with earlier years.
[b] Based on information drawn from the first two quarters of 1974.

information is given here about import activity. In so far as the purchase of new and the repair of existing machines are substitute activities, the comparison of current purchases is meaningful. A more useful comparison would perhaps be that between the sale of parts and the stock of metal working machines, but unfortunately this is not possible, as compatible information is not available. The observed ratio of parts to complete machines obviously will change over time, with the size and age of the stock of machines and, less meaningfully, with the concentration of firms in the engineering industry (which affects the ratio of inter- to intra-firm transactions).

The two series differ considerably from each other with regard to the information they give. While the *Business Monitor* figures indicate a very strong upward trend in the ratio of parts to complete machines, the *Census of Production* shows a very stable ratio of just over 10 per cent. The *Business Monitor* data are subject to important discontinuities where the coverage of firms or the classification has changed. The main change came in the fourth quarter of 1971, and this makes the later data very difficult to compare with the pre-1972 figures. The information recorded in Table 3.2 is taken straight from *Business Monitor*. Although information for the fourth quarter of 1971 was available on both the new and the old basis, no attempt was made to adjust the pre-1972 series, because the changes were considered too fundamental: numerical-control machines were omitted, [1] there was a change in the coverage of firms, and sales, rather than deliveries, were recorded. Although the aggregate information about complete machines was roughly consistent in both the *Business Monitor* and *Census of Production*, the information about parts (and hence the ratio of parts to complete machines) was not.

Even information about purchases of parts is, for a number of reasons, seriously deficient for our purposes. First, new parts may simply be replacements for identical parts that have become worn or broken. This type of change will alter the decline of the machine along its depreciation curve, but it will not alter the vintage of the machine unless the part is technically superior to the one it replaces. Second, metal working machines form only a part of the capital stock. Third, the figures are only for inter-firm transactions, although the major modifications may be designed and incorporated by the firm itself. Finally, these figures overlook the case of wholly rebuilt machines. [2]

Table 3.3

*Census of Production*: reconditioned metal working machines (£ thousand)

| Year | Reconditioned machines | All[a] machines | Ratio (per cent) |
|------|------------------------|-----------------|------------------|
| 1948 | 1,544 | 36,073 | 4·28 |
| 1951 | 2,992 | 54,453 | 5·49 |
| 1954 | 2,897 | 73,809 | 3·92 |
| 1958 | 2,478 | 79,632 | 3·11 |
| 1963 | 3,808 | 127,095 | 2·99 |
| 1968 | 4,017 | 172,609 | 2·33 |

[a] All metal-cutting and forming machines, except welding and physio-chemical.

What little evidence there is about rebuilt metal working machines is reported in Table 3.3. The data relate to the output of a part of the machine-tool industry (MLH 332), and, again, intra-firm activities and activities outside the industry are not covered. Also, nothing is known about the completeness of the rebuilding – whether the machines are simply repaired, are slightly modified, or are changed entirely, so as to conform to the latest specifications. The rather low percentage of activity in rebuilding machines cannot be taken as conclusive evidence that it is not important. The declining percentage of rebuilt machines to total sales will almost certainly reflect the level of concentration in the engineering industry (i.e. the ratio of inter- to intra-firm activities) just as much as any change in the propensity to rebuild machines.

There is also the question of cutting tools for the machines. Here is a case where a part of the machine is designed to be changed regularly. Senker et al. (1975, p. 6) point out that different tools enable general-purpose machines to produce different products. Toolmaking is certainly a major industrial activity, but data deficiencies would not allow Senker et al. (1975, p. 21) to be more exact than to estimate the combined 'in-house' and 'contract' toolmaking net output at between £60 million and £200 million per annum. For most types of machines such tools have not remained unchanged over time. Bell (1972, p. 74) and Senker et al. (1975) record some of the changes that have occurred in the tools.

The technical changes may be classified according to degree. They range from simple replacement of a worn-out part (with no change to remainder of the machine and, probably, no radical impact on the machine's productivity) to complete rebuilding (where every out-of-date part is replaced, resulting in the machine being as efficient as the very latest vintage). The two extremes represent situations that can fairly easily be integrated within the schema. Intermediate stages, where mixes of vintages result, are likely to pose more fundamental problems.

*Acquisitions and disposals of second-hand plant and machinery*

Traditional vintage theory has assumed the *ex ante* function to be the locus of points that are the most technically efficient at the time the investment is made. Johansen suggested that a positive study may have to acknowledge the existence of a number of *ex ante* functions, but that the efficient envelope of such functions may still broadly correspond with the accepted view of the relationship.

UK investment data from the *Census of Production* indicates that in practice the *ex ante* choices may be complicated. The disposal data reported in Table 3.4 show that UK engineering industries sell some proportion of their capital stock. While there is no direct evidence that they purchase second-hand plant and machinery, this seems likely to be the case. The available data also suggest that trading in older vintages is likely to be more important for certain types of capital than for others (for example, relatively more important for vehicles than for plant and machinery).

Table 3.4

*Census of Production*: acquisitions and disposals of investment goods (£ million)

| Industry group | Plant and machinery | | | | Vehicles | | | |
|---|---|---|---|---|---|---|---|---|
| | 1963 | | 1968 | | 1963 | | 1968 | |
| | A | D | A | D | A | D | A | D |
| Mechanical and instrument engineering | 75·3 | 5·6 | 123·0 | 10·0 | 10·7 | 4·1 | 19·3 | 6·8 |
| Electrical engineering | 53·4 | 5·2 | 74·4 | 3·9 | 5·3 | 1·7 | 7·2 | 2·6 |
| Motor vehicles | 63·8 | 1·3 | 71·8 | 2·9 | 2·9 | 1·2 | 3·8 | 1·7 |
| Aircraft | 10·9 | 2·2 | 26·3 | 1·2 | 0·8 | 0·2 | 1·7 | 0·3 |
| Other vehicles | 2·3 | 0·4 | 3·6 | 0·4 | 0·4 | 0·1 | 0·4 | 0·1 |
| Metal goods not elsewhere specified | 32·7 | 2·0 | 49·7 | 3·1 | 7·6 | 2·8 | 8·6 | 3·3 |
| Shipbuilding and marine engineering | 11·2 | 1·5 | 11·9 | 0·6 | 0·9 | 0·3 | 0·6 | 0·2 |

A = acquisitions; D = disposals.

Activity at the intensive margin will involve reviewing the *ex ante* functions of all vintages, although an adjustment of the functions to account for depreciation will play an increasingly important part the older is the vintage under consideration. Gaps in the function will appear where vintages with certain characteristics are not available. The impact of second-hand trading on the other Johansen concepts is much less marked. The short-run macro function, for example, depends only on the stocks of various production units held by the industry at a particular time, and not on the transition from one stock to another.

*Evidence of technical change at the intensive margin*

The implication of the simple embodiment and 'fixity' hypotheses appears to be that new capital (i.e. the most modern) should be more efficient than the capital already in use. Johansen (1972, p. 9) points out that such a situation assumes the existence of a single *ex ante* function where know-how is freely available everywhere to everyone who is interested. Where this is not the case, there will exist a whole nest of *ex ante* functions, and observations drawn from the real world about the intensive margin will be characterised by a variety of technical efficiencies. Of course, some of these production units may not survive in the long run, but can exist in the short run.

Evidence about the vintage hypothesis is scarce. Verdoorn's law, for example, gives some support for the vintage hypothesis but it is not direct proof. The positive relationship between the rate of growth of productivity and the rate of growth of output may be caused by high levels of investment in the latest vintage by rapidly growing industries. Continuing in this vein, Wabe (1973, p. 38) has suggested that an industry with no growth (or even negative growth) in output will experience productivity change from replacement of obsolete equipment (or scrapping of obsolete equipment with no replacement). The vintage hypothesis thereby suggests the possibility of a U-shaped relationship for the Verdoorn regression. So far, only Helps (1974) has tested this hypothesis and has provided tentative empirical evidence of a non-symmetrical U-shaped function. However, the evidence is in many ways poor, because if the vintage hypothesis is correct the Verdoorn relationship is misspecified.

Few studies have looked into the possibility of estimating vintage functions where capital of different vintages appear directly in the function. One reason is that there rarely exists information that is sufficiently detailed for a function of this type to be estimated. A general reaction is to attempt to make use of rather aggregate published investment data. Heathfield (1972b) has isolated a model where aggregate output per head is a function of cumulative past investment, capital usage and a time trend. Fair (1971) has isolated a model, estimated as an employment function, where the change in full capacity employment is a function of the change in full-capacity output, the wage–rental ratio and a time trend. The estimated function is again obtained by aggregation over vintages and, although the results relate to two fairly detailed industry groups, they appear a long way removed from the micro vintage models.

The most incisive evidence is likely to come from direct observation of 'best-practice' and 'average' production units. Salter (1966, pp. 48–50 and 95–9) summarises some information of this type, but the evidence he provides is suggestive rather than conclusive. Only his Table 9 (ibid., p. 96), which relates to the beet and cement industries, links productivity to the age of plant. Even here nothing is known about the role played by increased capital intensity, which might be independent of vintage effects. The remaining data is even less conclusive. While Salter's Table 11 (ibid., p. 98) indicates that productivity growth was faster in industries that undertook important modifications to their capital stock, it again fails to distinguish growth in the capital–labour ratio from vintage effects. Tables 5 and 10 in Salter (1966, pp. 48 and 97) give information about 'best-practice' and 'average' production units. Although it is tempting to interpret the difference in efficiency between the 'best-practice' and 'the average' production units as the result of lags in the adoption of up-to-date technologies, this has not been proven.

All of the Salter evidence points towards the existence of embodied technological progress (although the phenomenon would appear to be more important in some industries than others), but the evidence is only suggestive. Gregory and James (1973) attempted to provide a more substantial test of the vintage hypothesis. Their results, which are the most important to date, are not favourable to the vintage hypothesis. Their evidence, drawn from Australian manufacturing industries in the mid-1950s, involved a comparison of the efficiency of new factories with the average efficiency of existing establishments in the same industry. They concluded that the average age of factories is not important in explaining variations in value-added per worker between establishments within a given industry, with the implication that it is not possible to automatically associate new factories with best practice techniques. In addition, the results indicate that vintage effects are quantitatively insignificant as an explanation of cross-sectional productivity dispersion in most industries (or indeed over time for a given industry) and that, although vintage effects may be important in a few industries, the number of such industries is likely to be small.

Haig (1975, pp. 378–9) argues that the Gregory and James results are by no means conclusive. The ratio of average labour productivity of new to existing plant is about 1·10 to 1·18 (depending on the approach adopted). The 95 per cent confidence intervals for the 1·10 ratio are 0·98 and 1·23, which range from an almost zero to a strongly positive vintage effect. Haig notes that other sources of evidence suggest an average lag of seven years between the best-practice and industry average. This implies a productivity difference of about 25 per cent, which is not very far removed from the upper boundary of the confidence interval.

Gregory and James (1973, p. 1144) felt that there was little enough evidence that new factories were more efficient than established production units, but said that what little differential there was could be partly explained by the greater size of new factories (quite independently of vintage effects). Haig (1975, p. 379) criticised the use of value-added as a measure of size. He favoured a measure of firm size based on the number of employees, and found that, using the same functional form, the coefficient on size became insignificantly different from zero. However, Gregory and James (1975, pp. 384–6) pointed out that the main results do not depend on the proof of this relationship; value-added is a theoretically more valid measure; employment measures of firm size *bias* the slope coefficient downwards; and, even if an employment-based measure is used, the relationship remains significant if a log-linear or semi-log formulation is adopted.

One final point that Haig (1975, pp. 380-1) dealt with was the possibility that the prices of output from new factories are forced downwards in an attempt to break into a market controlled by existing production units; but, as Gregory and James (1975, p. 387) point out, no evidence exists to support this hypothesis or to refute it.

With regard to existing production units, it is important to note that, in addition to the embodied technical change that they experience when replacing and adding to their capital stocks, they experience disembodied technical change, through which they accumulate gains in productivity, in the gestation period between the date when the new plant is planned and the date at which it achieves its planned performance. [3] The date at which plans are formalised may *precede* the opening of the factory by a number of years, and the associated threat of new competition may induce existing units to search for and to introduce changes in order to remain competitive or to remove the new source of competition.

The Gregory and James study looked at a single snapshot from the dynamic process of technical change, but embodied changes may dry up at any time. Work on demand-induced technical change (see, for example, Schmookler, 1966) suggests that expectations or experience of a recession may cause a cutback in R & D in investment-goods industries. In addition, other authors (see Ruttan, 1959) have argued that major innovations or clusters of innovations may follow one another after quite long intervals, and these changes may be associated with specific pieces of equipment such as computers and machine tools. Under these conditions, embodied changes may, at a given time, be quantitatively insignificant compared with disembodied changes, but this may not be true at all times.

There are a number of other problems that neither Haig nor Gregory and James considered. The first is that a cross-industry regression is unlikely to yield any insights about the empirical validity of the concept of increasing returns to scale. Optimal firm size may well vary significantly from industry to industry, and the question of returns to scale should be considered by comparing plants of different sizes within a given industry. The second point is that the linear formulation that both Haig and Gregory and James adopt may give misleading results. Unless returns to scale are ever-increasing, it is likely that a quadratic function will prove more realistic. If the actual function has quadratic form, then it is by no means certain that the large average size of firms in the sample works in favour of higher productivity. Indivisibilities of plant, industrial concentration and goals other than profit maximisation may result in greater-than-optimal firm size and lower-than-maximum productivity. Such factors may offset even potentially large gains from embodied technical change. This may also be one explanation for the fact that, in about half of the new factories, labour productivity was lower than the industry average.

Gregory and James had insufficient data to estimate their regression equation for each industry in turn. However, they were able, using the 1969 Australian census data, to make a simple comparison of firm size and productivity for different industries. For existing firms, productivity often is not a monotonically increasing function of firm size. The examples given in Table 3.5 show that the largest firms

## Table 3.5

## Productivity of various industry groups, by firm size

(a) *Cement products*[a]

| Industry group | Firms with 10–19 employees | Firms with 20–49 employees | Firms with 50–99 employees | Firms with 100 or more employees | All firms |
|---|---|---|---|---|---|
| Ready-mixed concrete | 9·97 | – | – | – | 12·87 |
| Concrete pipe | 7·95 | 8·25 | 8·33 | 7·15 | 7·81 |
| Concrete products (excluding pipes) | 5·88 | 6·90 | 7·48 | 7·16 | 6·36 |
| Asbestos cement products | – | – | – | – | 7·48 |
| All industries shown | – | – | – | – | – |

(b) *Industrial chemicals*[b]

| Industry group | Firms with 10–19 employees | Firms with 20–49 employees | Firms with 50–99 employees | Firms with 100 or more employees | All firms |
|---|---|---|---|---|---|
| Chemical fertilisers | – | 6·90 | 12·40 | 11·81 | 11·77 |
| Industrial gases | – | – | – | – | – |
| Synthetic resins and synthetic rubber | 11·69 | 16·32 | 12·28 | 16·12 | 15·25 |
| Organic industrial chemicals not elsewhere specified | – | 9·98 | 17·08 | 11·53 | 13·99 |
| Inorganic industrial chemicals not elsewhere specified | – | – | – | – | – |
| All industries shown | 13·57 | 9·53 | 13·73 | 12·00 | 12·24 |

(c) *Motor vehicles*[c]

| Industry group | Firms with 10–19 employees | Firms with 20–49 employees | Firms with 50–99 employees | Firms with 100 or more employees | All firms |
|---|---|---|---|---|---|
| Motor vehicles | – | 7·21 | – | 8·22 | 8·19 |
| Truck and bus bodies, etc. | 4·48 | 4·80 | 5·03 | 4·67 | 4·68 |
| Motor-vehicle instruments and electrics | – | 4·20 | – | 4·31 | 4·29 |
| Motor-vehicle parts not elsewhere specified | 4·90 | 4·81 | 5·05 | 5·42 | 5·28 |
| All industries shown | 4·66 | 4·99 | 5·46 | 7·15 | 6·86 |

[a] Cement itself is omitted leaving the Australian Standard Industrial Classification Order (ASIC) subgroups 2832–5.

[b] Taken to be basic chemicals: ASIC 2711–5.

[c] Taken to be total motor vehicles and parts: ASIC 3211–4.

– Indicates that the information for the corresponding cell is not published individually, although it appears in the ASIC total.

Source: 'Manufacturing establishments: selected items of data classified by industry and employment size', *Economic Census 1968/9*, Commonwealth Bureau of Censuses and Statistics, Canberra.

(those reporting 100 or more employees) often experience lower productivity than do smaller firms in the same industry; and in some industries (for instance, the concrete pipe, organic chemicals and truck and bus body industries) their average productivity is below the average for the industry as a whole. In addition, in five out of the seven cases where information is given for firms with 50–99 employees, productivity is higher for this group than for firms with 100 or more employees. Added to this is the tendency for larger firms to be more capital intensive. Had this been taken into account, the productivity figures would have been even lower for the larger firms.

Despite Gregory and James's claim (1973, p. 1140) that their industry breakdown was detailed, the aggregate nature of some of their industry groups presents a further problem. The census data used in Table 3.5 conceal the fact that, due to intra-group variations in the nature of products and production technologies, labour productivities may vary greatly within a given industry group, and even for firms of the same size. This applies even if the sample is limited to firms employing more than ten workers (see ibid., p. 1139). The range of variation is increased even further if we look across establishments of different sizes as well as over product types within an industry group.

It appears from the results summarised in Table 3.5 that all of the industries experience wide ranges of productivity. Expressing these ranges as the ratio of the highest to the lowest productivity, the ratios calculated from Table 1 in the Gregory and James study (for the new factory sample) are 3·96 for cement products and 7·20 for industrial chemicals (the range for motor vehicles was not available). The productivity ranges calculated for existing factories from Table 3.5 are 2·18 for cement products, 2·80 for industrial chemicals and 1·96 for motor vehicles. Even if firm size is held constant, the variation is still large, with a maximum ratio of 1·70 for cement products (10–19-employee group), 2·68 for industrial chemicals (20–49-employee group), and 1·91 for motor vehicles (100-plus group). Close to half the variation in productivity isolated by Gregory and James can be accounted for in this way, even though the industry and firm-size categories reported here are still aggregates. In addition, no attempt has been made to account for differences caused by regional conditions. If new plants are established in both relatively high and relatively low labour-cost areas, this will affect the range of productivities experienced.

The review presented here of the existing literature indicates that there is an urgent need for further empirical research. Perhaps the most incisive evidence will prove to be direct observation of new and old factories. Given a more appropriate sample of new firms than could be constructed from the Salter data, the approach adopted by Gregory and James could, with some improvements, prove a useful first step in establishing which industries are characterised to any extent by vintage effects. The criticisms outlined here suggest that the sample should be based on more disaggregated industry groups, be stratified by region, and have sufficient observations to enable the nature of 'returns to scale' to be established for each industry. With such a sample, the difficulties of isolating the importance of vintage effects would be greatly reduced.

A major body of evidence often used against the vintage hypothesis concerns the fact that neoclassical production functions invariably explain the empirical 'facts of life' so well that the alternative (vintage) formulations are redundant. The work of Layard et al. (1971) is a particularly relevant example of this type of evidence, as it is a cross-sectional study of plants in the electrical engineering industry. The results of this study indicate that neoclassical functions fit well and are characterised by a high degree of substitution between factors (i.e. the isoquants appear to be almost straight lines). From this evidence Layard et al. (1971, p. 20) draw important normative conclusions about the role and intensity of manpower planning.

There have been a number of attempts to incorporate elements of vintage theory in the traditional neoclassical framework. For example, Griliches and Ringstad (1971, p. 29) attempted, on the basis of establishment data, to pick up embodiment effects using a traditional CES function but with dummies for each of the years when establishments were founded. They concluded (ibid., p. 67) that 'No clear pattern emerges for the "year of establishment" variables. Given our data we are unable to detect any "embodiment" effects.' However, many of the comments made above about the Gregory and James study apply equally to this study, and it is not too surprising that no pervasive pattern was found. A study by Hildebrand and Liu (1965) was more favourable to the vintage hypothesis. They weighted the capital variable by the ratio of net to gross book value of capital in order to account for variations in depreciation and age. Where investment causes the ratio of net to gross values to differ, both the capital elasticity and the returns to scale are considerably larger. This is taken to indicate that the modernisation of equipment plays an important role. Although some evidence can be found to support the vintage hypothesis, this approach lacks theoretical rigour, and the variables used to summarise the vintage effects have not always performed well. The results obtained have failed to give any real impetus to empirical work based on more theoretically rigorous vintage models.

In the light of the apparent success of the neoclassical models, it is interesting to ask whether the Johansen approach can provide an explanation for the existing body of empirical results. Substitution in the schema arises from the diversity of tasks that any particular piece of equipment can undertake. In this way there exists the possibility of substitution, but of a much more limited kind than is assumed in the neoclassical models. The universe of machine tasks may, for example, include sets $A$, $B$ and $C$, denoting tasks performed by three different machines (for instance, milling, planing and broaching machines). The size of any particular set relative to the universe of tasks is an indication of the degree of specialisation of the machine. In so far as the sets intersect, there may exist a subset of tasks that can be performed on any of the machines. In this sense, a limited degree of substitution is possible between the machines. The implication of the simplest form of the Johansen schema is that we may analyse substitution between machines of different types if we reduce the set of operations from the universe as a whole to a subset that is common to all machines in the sample. Champernowne (1953–54) suggested that technologies that are not substitutes can nonetheless be made to look like substitutes by a chain-linking process. Suppose that for one subset of machine tasks $A$ and $B$ are substitutes, and for a different subset $B$ and $C$ are substitutes. $A$ and $C$, however, are not substitutes and can be compared only through their common link $B$. In this case, chain-linking may not prove a meaningful exercise.

The Johansen schema can generate two-input short-run macro functions with neoclassical properties. Inputs are measured in real terms and disaggregated into sufficiently detailed groups to be internally homogeneous. [4] If a meaningful common measure of different types of capital can be found, then it is possible to treat capital as a current input. In the two-factor case, the *ex ante* function can be written

$$\tilde{Y} = f(\tilde{K}, \tilde{L}) \tag{3.1}$$

and for simplicity, omitting the vintage subscripts, the *ex post* functions appear as

$$Y_j = \frac{1}{\xi_j^K} K_j = \frac{1}{\xi_j^L} L_j \tag{3.2}$$

The short-run macro function can now be summarised in linear programming form as

maximise

$$Y = \sum_j Y_j$$

subject to

$$S^K \geq \sum_j \xi_j^K Y_j$$

$$S^L \geq \sum_j \xi_j^L Y_j$$

$$Y_j \geq 0$$

and

$$K_j, L_j, S^K, S^L \geq 0 \tag{3.3}$$

where $Y_j > 0$ implies that $K_j > 0$, through the assumption of constant returns to scale, and the upper limit, $\tilde{Y}_j$, is now subsumed in the first inequality.

The essence of the Johansen proof of the nature of the short-run macro function for this two-input case, $Y = F(K, L)$, can be demonstrated in diagram form. $G(r, w)$, shown in Figure 3.1, represents the set of established, technically feasible and economically viable points. $Z$ represents the zero quasi-rent line. The total (industry) output of all production units in this region, $Y_1$, is found by double integration (over $\xi^K$ and $\xi^L$ consistent with the non-negative quasi-rent condition). Total input demands for the industry, $K$ and $L$, are found in a similar way (i.e. by integration of the input–output coefficients weighted by the level of output).

The situation we are interested in concerns what happens to total input demands where relative factor prices change (i.e. $r_1/w_1 \rightarrow r_2/w_2$ while output is maintained at the level $Y_1$. Figure 3.2 illustrates the possible outcomes. If we suppose that

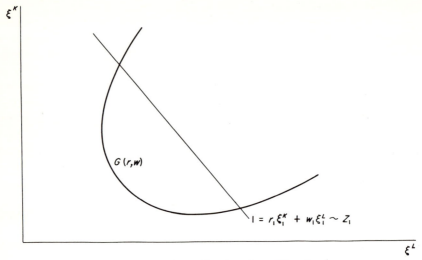

$1 = r_1 \xi_1^K + w_1 \xi_1^L \sim Z_1$

Fig. 3.1 The utilised region, $G(r, w)$

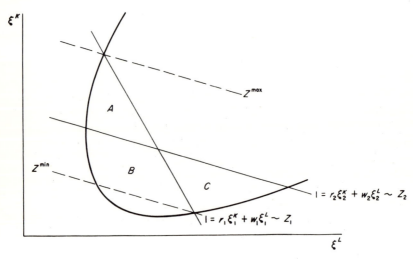

$Z^{max}$

$A$

$Z^{min}$

$B$

$C$

$1 = r_2 \xi_2^K + w_2 \xi_2^L \sim Z_2$

$1 = r_1 \xi_1^K + w_1 \xi_1^L \sim Z_1$

Fig. 3.2 Derivation of the isoquant

36

relative factor prices are given autonomously, a change in relative prices from $r_1/w_1$ to $r_2/w_2$ is consistent with a wide range of zero quasi-rent lines, $Z$, as the absolute level of prices is not fixed. It can be shown, however, that $Z_2$ must lie between $Z^{\min}$ and $Z^{\max}$ if output is to remain at level $Y_1$. At $Z^{\max}$ no production units are lost but some are gained, while at $Z^{\min}$ none are gained but a number are lost. In between, there should exist a function $Z_2$ that creates a new half-space such that the output lost from the industry (from technologies in region $A$) is just compensated by the output gained (from production units whose technologies fall in region $C$). The technologies lost were relatively capital intensive and those gained were relatively labour intensive. The aggregate input demands must have been affected in such a way as to lower $K$ and raise $L$. The capital–labour ratio along the isoquant moves inversely with the rental–wage ratio – the key characteristic of neoclassical technologies.

The way now seems open to find the distributions $f(\xi^K, \xi^L)$ that are consistent with CES production functions. Unfortunately, a meaningful summary statistic of heterogeneous capital is not generally available. Johansen (1972, p. 8) suggests using a value measure of capital. This does not give rise to any real problems in the two-current- and one-fixed-input case where substitution between current inputs is being analysed. Where capital is treated as a current input and measured in value terms, changes in the zero quasi-rent line are reflected in changes in the valuation of capital and, hence, in the distribution $f(\xi^K, \xi^L)$. Under these circumstances the isoquant need not retain the desired neoclassical properties. The Johansen schema therefore cannot be used as an explanation of the neoclassical empirical results that have used a value measure of capital.

Johansen's very careful treatment of capital throughout his book indicates that he was very aware of the problems associated with the capital input. His preference was to treat every type of capital quite separately. Under these circumstances, the original representation of the schema, described by equations (2.7) above, is appropriate. If, again for simplicity, we omit the vintage subscripts, then the linear programming problem appears as

maximise

$$Y = \sum_j Y_j$$

subject to

$$S^i \geqq \sum_j \xi_j^i Y_j$$

$$\tilde{Y}_j \geqq Y_j \geqq 0$$

and

$$S^i, \xi_j^i \geqq 0 \tag{3.4}$$

The role played by capital is now summarised in the output inequality, because this can be expressed in terms of capital usage as

$$\frac{1}{\xi_{jv}^K} \tilde{K}_{jv} \geqq \frac{1}{\xi_{jv}^K} K_{jv} \geqq 0$$

This rigorous treatment of the capital input means that changes in relative factor prices, while holding output constant, produce movements around the isoquant in the $(\xi^1, \xi^2)$ plane concerned with current inputs, but movements from plane to plane in the case of capital. In practice, we might expect changes in capital types to cause a movement from plane to plane in terms of current inputs. To take a well-tried example, the skill and fuel requirements of a bulldozer are very different from those of a shovel. From an empirical point of view, however, theoretical rigour implies immense problems of measurement and estimation (see, for example, Pyatt, 1964b, pp. 24–5).

The current explanations of the neoclassical empirical results are reviewed in Chapter 8 below, where an alternative explanation is provided and some further comments are made about the 'measurement of capital' problem.

**The importance of perfect competition and profit-maximising behaviour to the Johansen schema: some initial thoughts on the effects of alternative market regimes and managerial behaviour**

*Profit maximisation under perfect competition*

The market regime that Johansen assumes to underlie all of the constructs is one of perfect competition in a single product market, and the theory is valid in a centrally planned economy intent on using resources in the most efficient manner.

It is interesting to point out some of the features of the Johansen short-run macro function. The primal problem is to maximise output subject to supply constraints and the condition of non-negative activity levels for each production unit. The choice of output maximisation appears unusual in a competitive model because it is not necessarily consistent with profit maximisation. It is appropriate in so far as the production problem is often phrased in terms of obtaining maximum output from given resources (a technically efficient relationship). More normally, however, we see the problem in the context of profit-maximising or cost-minimising behaviour in the light of a given technology.

Johansen avoids the potential inconsistency between the output- and profit-maximising results by assuming that factor rewards are equal to the shadow prices that appear in the solution to the dual problem. Full use is made of the link between linear programming and marginal analysis. In the output-maximising model, units along the separating plane earn zero quasi-rents; that is, on the basis of imputed prices, the marginal costs of production are set equal to the marginal revenues to which they give rise. This is the traditional profit-maximising result.

The short-run macro function, however, relates to an industry or sector defined in terms of the product market. The industry may not, however, be an appropriate level of aggregation when analysing factor markets. If, for example, the labour market is wider than the industry, the going wage rate may be determined by market supply and demand and imposed on the industry. In so far as these rates differ from the shadow prices found in the solution to the dual problem, cost-minimising and output-maximising behaviour will give different results.

The more general way of specifying the model is to assume profit-maximising behaviour. Thus, the model transforms into the more traditional constrained profit-maximising behaviour.

Maximise

$$\Pi = pY - \sum_j \sum_v \sum_i c^i \xi^i_{jv} Y_{jv} \tag{3.5}$$

subject to inequalities (3.4)

where $p$ is the price per unit of output and $c^i$ is the price per unit of the $i$th input. In this way it is possible to isolate the inputs, $K$ and $L$, that satisfy the short-run macro function $Y = F(K, L)$.

The short-run macro function is, however, an industry-level model; and, at this level of aggregation, product prices will generally not be constant at different levels of output. As the industry constitutes the sole source of supply of the product, the demand curve may be assumed to be downward sloping to the right in the price–quantity space. In a simple model of labour supply, whether the wage rate is constant will depend on the size of the industry demand relative to total demand for that factor.

In so far as the industry constitutes an important part of total market demand for any particular input, increases in its level of activity will tend to bid up the price of inputs. Changes in products and factor prices can be incorporated in the programming case quite easily. By making $p = p(Y)$ and $c = c(Y)$, where $p'(Y) < 0$ and $c'(Y) > 0$ (which are the first differentials with respect to output), we can include a downward-sloping industry-demand curve with an upward-sloping supply curve for any particular input. As Baumol and Quandt (1963, pp. 437–8) point out, this generalisation means that the objective function has terms $Y \cdot p(Y)$ and $Y \cdot c(Y)$ and that the expression will generally be non-linear. Given knowledge of the demand and supply functions, an iterative procedure can be used to obtain a solution. At each level of $Y$, both $p$ and $c$ are constants, and the problem remains one of selecting a set of activity levels, $\{Y_{jv}\}$, that maximise profits.

*Profit maximisation under alternative market regimes*

In the following analysis it is assumed that the optimal level of $Y^*$ chosen is less than or equal to $\tilde{Y}$. In addition, for simplicity we adopt the assumptions that $p'(Y) < 0$ and $c'(Y) = 0$. It can be shown that the short-run macro function is identical in both the competitive and monopoly situations under conditions of profit maximisation given a distribution of established technologies $f(\xi^K, \xi^L)$. The choice of activity levels, $\{Y_{jv}\}$, and the overall level of industry output, $Y^*$, that will appear in equilibrium will, however, be different. It is also argued that intermediate degrees of imperfect competition are more difficult to handle.

*Competition.* If it is assumed that there are a large number and a varied distribution of production units, the marginal-cost curve for the industry is the sum of the same

39

curves for individual firms, and the equilibrium level of output is determined by supply equal to demand at the output level $Y^c$. At this level quasi-rents are zero on the marginal units. This is the worst position that can be tolerated: the whole of the revenue that accrues from operating the marginal unit is 'consumed' by the variable costs of running it.

As firms are induced to introduce their most efficient vintages first (and their least efficient last), given constant price per unit of input, marginal cost is a non-decreasing function of output. At very low levels of output, the marginal unit has the same characteristics as all other units currently in use, and, therefore, marginal and average variable costs coincide. As output rises, less and less efficient units are brought into use and marginal costs increase. Average variable costs are pulled upwards, but lag behind marginal costs because the units from which the average is calculated are all at least as efficient as the marginal unit and in some cases are more efficient.

So long as the units in use are characterised by more than one level of efficiency, the non-decreasing form of the marginal-cost function opens up a gap between the marginal-cost and average-variable-cost functions. If this gap is not filled by the average fixed costs at $Y^c$ then firms in the industry can earn transitory profits. The equilibrium level of output, $Y^c$, is assured whether short-run profits are positive or negative (i.e. whether average total costs pass above or below average revenue at $Y^c$), because some production units are earning positive quasi-rents and are thus contributing to their sunk costs.

In the case of perfect competition, the output of the industry is quite simply the sum of all output activities carried out on production units earning non-negative quasi-rents in the light of the current demand situation. The programming problem is one of maximising profits subject to the technical constraints, non-negative activity levels and production units earning non-negative quasi-rents.

*Monopoly.* The case of the monopolist is just as simple given the single aim of maximising profits. The equilibrium level of output, $Y^m$, is determined by the intersection of the marginal-revenue and marginal-cost curves. The price charged by the monopolist is higher and the output supplied is lower than in the competitive industry. It is an interesting result of the static analysis that the monopolist will tend to lay up a greater part of his capital stock. Under price and factor cost expectations where these inefficient vintages are never expected to do better, the monopolist may scrap capital earlier and employ a smaller (though, on average, more efficient) capital stock than would a group of competitive firms.

The programming problem is one of maximising profits subject to the technical constraints, non-negative activity levels, and marginal revenue greater than or equal to marginal costs. If the monopolist were to reduce his level of profits towards zero (under the threat of potential competition, for example), the industry equilibrium would at some point reach (and possibly pass) $Y^m = Y^c$.

*Other market regimes.* Generalisation of the market regimes to the intermediate states of oligopoly and monopolistic competition appears more difficult to effect. In such cases the essential problem is to find some means of determining the market shares of firms in the industry at given levels of output for the industry. Once this is known, profit-maximising behaviour can be used to allocate output among production units owned by each firm. The allocation of demand between firms in an oligopolistic market will depend on the type of oligopoly (i.e. collusive or non-collusive), the nature of competition (i.e. price of quality) and the manner in which each firm's product characteristics are decided upon (for instance, a process akin to game theory or price leadership). In principle some form of allocative model determining market shares can be devised for a particular regime and spliced onto the system, which would then function broadly as before.

*Alternative theories of managerial behaviour*

At this stage, however, it seems more important to assess the implications that managerial and behavioural theories of the firm have for the schema. Managerial theories suggest that, given market power, the objective function may take a form other than profit maximisation. The most commonly cited is sales-revenue maximisation. Behavioural theories, on the other hand, suggest that firms may be controlled by management intent on 'satisficing', which only under extreme conditions collapses to profit maximisation.

*Managerial theories.* Here, the analysis is limited to Baumol's sales-revenue maximisation hypothesis (Baumol, 1959). This simple model is sufficient to give a flavour of the implications of alternative managerial theories for the equilibrium result. Given the static nature of the short-run macro function, the dynamic (see Mueller, 1967, and Marris, 1971) managerial theories do not appear particularly relevant to this part of the schema. The assumption of sales-revenue maximisation subject to a profit constraint results in a slightly more complicated programming problem:

maximise $pY$

subject to inequalities (3.4)

and

$$\sum_j \sum_v \sum_i (pY_{jv} - c^i \zeta^i_{jv} Y_{jv} - AD_j) \geqq \Pi^{\min} \qquad (3.6)$$

where $AD$ denotes the level of advertising expenditure. Advertising plays an integral role in the revenue-maximisation model. Baumol allowed advertising expenditure to affect the level of output, but not the price of the product. Under these conditions, it is possible to raise the level of output without reducing price: the extra expenditure on advertising induces additional consumption at the same price. Sandmeyer (1964) and Haveman and DeBartolo (1968) have modified the Baumol model in order to allow advertising to affect both price and quantity. This again further complicates the relationships underlying the objective function but, in principle, the solution can be found in the same way.

One case of particular interest concerns the equilibrium position where marginal cost is greater than average revenue and average revenue is greater than marginal revenue. Expansion after the point where marginal cost is equal to marginal revenue reduces profits but continues to expand revenue. Expansion after the point where marginal cost is equal to average revenue (anywhere up to the point where average total cost is equal to average revenue, i.e. profits are zero) is achieved by employing capital that, under a profit-maximising goal, would be laid up. The monopolist finances the losses made on operating wholly inefficient capital from the pool of profits made from more efficient units.

*Behavioural theories.* In the behavioural approach, the firm is seen essentially as a coalition of individuals and groups. Each group tends to be concerned with a different (although obviously related) aspect of the organisation, and hence has its own goals. For this reason, the behavioural theory has tended to specify a fairly large number of managerial goals. Cyert and March (1963), for example, distinguish five: production goal, inventory goal, sales goal, market-share goal, and profit goal. Cohen and Cyert (1965, p. 338) also argue that this is the optimal number of goals to specify.

Because different parts of the organisation are associated with different goals, they will often be inconsistent. In attempting to eradicate inconsistencies (which the behavioural theory suggests will not be wholly successful), the various groups within the coalition will be brought into conflict. If decision making is to achieve a clearly formulated goal, such inconsistencies and conflicts must be eliminated. But, as Wildsmith (1973, p. 24) points out, if this is true of 'economic man' it certainly is not true of 'organisational man'. Cyert and March (1963) argue that the goals that evolve are imperfectly rationalised and tend to be stated in the form of aspiration levels rather than maximising constraints. The behavioural theory does not centre on a unique objective of the firm, and the objectives that are considered strategic are not formulated in terms of a maximisation hypothesis.

A major problem is that on dropping explicit maximisation from the analysis the possibility of deriving simple and elegant solutions that describe the position of the firm at any particular time becomes more remote. Although the concept of the capacity region remains relevant, its derivation from the *ex ante* functions and the manner in which it collapses to the short-run macro function are no longer obvious. Failure to include an explicit maximand makes all of the concepts more difficult to handle. Wildsmith (1973, p. 30) notes that 'non-maximising models may offer useful insights, but they will be ultimately unsatisfactory if they fail to yield identifiable equilibrium conditions'.

Although the behavioural theories drop the use of an explicit maximand, Baumol (1965, p. 297) has argued that the limited, sequential, problem-oriented search procedure suggested by the theory may be consistent with an implicit form of optimisation of a deeper kind. Search is now seen as having a positive cost and being subject to diminishing returns. Baumol sees the firm as acting in an 'optimally imperfect' manner if it seeks a point where the additional costs of change are just balanced by the additional advantages gained. Such an approach is adopted in Chapter 4 in an attempt to derive a unique *ex ante* function from the more realistic concept of an *ex ante* region.

Profit maximisation was central to the Johansen thesis and behavioural aspects played little or no role. As Wildsmith (1973, p. 34) points out, 'Profit maximisation in such circumstances is not so much a behavioural assumption as a necessary condition for survival. . . . The problems arising from considering the firm as an administrative and social organisation are not relevant.' Behavioural theory does not play a dominant role in this book, despite the one or two attempts at incorporating certain aspects of it into later chapters.


**Notes**

[1] If numerical control machines are added back into the post-1971 totals, the parts–total ratios become 12·89, 13·71 and 15·11 per cent (as against 13·73, 14·66 and 16·20 per cent). The new ratios are not very different from the old, even though they assume that the purchase of parts for numerical control machines is zero (because no information about these parts is available). The main changes are from the other two sources.

[2] A number of companies have special divisions wholly concerned with re-building machines.

[3] Both Salter (1966, pp. 83–99) and Svennilson (1964) have stressed the co-existence of embodied and disembodied technical changes.

[4] Hahn and Matthews (1964, p. 110) point out that 'As far as pure theory is concerned the "measurement of capital" is no problem at all because we never have to face it if we do not choose to. With our armchair omniscience we can account for each machine separately.'

# 4   The ex ante function

## Introduction

The *ex ante* function is a key link in the integrated production system and plays an important role in putty–clay vintage theory. In the forms in which it has usually appeared, however, it can be criticised as naïve. The function conceived by Johansen (1959, 1972), Salter (1966) and Svennilson (1964) is represented in the input–output space by a unique set of points the locus of which is a production relationship exhibiting classical properties. [1] The function outlined in Johansen's 1972 study is the most sophisticated in so far as it distinguishes different input categories for each type of machine (where no meaningful common units of measure exist). In his 1959 study, Johansen had suggested that the dimensions of the *ex ante* function should be restricted by taking into account national (or regional) supplies of factors. In 1972, however, he was more concerned about the assumption that knowledge is freely available, and concluded that in a positive study it may be necessary to distinguish a large number of *ex ante* functions (up to one for each entrepreneur), while in a normative study it may be possible to consider the efficient envelope of such functions. The comments made above in Chapter 3 suggest that activity at the intensive margin may involve purchases of older vintages, which may severely complicate the *ex ante* concept. All these generalisations appear to leave the function basically unsound.

Harcourt (1972, p. 56) has argued that the degree of *ex ante* substitution may be extremely small. Nevertheless, he concedes that we could allow each industry a small arc of techniques from which to choose. If this is the case, we can use Sato's proof (see his 1974 study) to show that the *ex ante* function possesses the desired neoclassical properties; but this is not the main problem. The important question-mark hanging over the function concerns the intermediate technologies that are not in use but can be developed given R & D resources. The question of how much R & D, raised by Johansen (1972, p. 9) indicates that there exists a further, and so far largely ignored, dimension to the *ex ante* function. The technology can no longer be described by a single function. It is a set of points having positive breadth (i.e. in the north-east/south-west direction). Movements within the region have costs and benefits that make the R & D decision endogenous.

The model developed below is based on an industry with a large number of firms. At any given time, each firm has a set of technologies at various stages of readiness. The corpus of knowledge available to any particular firm is conditioned by its own unique history and no two firms need be faced by the same set of technologies. The *ex ante* choices range from processes already used by the firm, through those used by other firms, to those at a pilot stage or even further removed from everyday use.

Each technology is associated with a probability distribution of future net revenues, and this will depend on a wide variety of factors (for instance, R & D costs, the time allowed for R & D, movements in factor and product prices, changes in consumer tastes, and trade-union attitudes to various production activities). This chapter demonstrates that the traditional descriptions of the *ex ante* concept gloss over very complex dynamic adjustment processes when they assume unique, classically shaped functions. Although no succinct mathematical proof is given, it is shown that, when the range of possible outcomes is diffuse, induced technical change is unlikely to give rise to a function with the appearance of a well-defined *ex ante* frontier.

## The ex ante region and the T-isocost family

The assumption of exogenously given *ex ante* functions, each one unique at a given time and possessing classical properties, greatly simplifies the construction of growth models (see, for example, the models of Johansen, 1959, and Svennilson 1964). However, attempts to endogenise technical progress, [2] and research aimed at establishing the nature of the production function associated with the output of inventions, [3] indicate that an *ex ante* region may be more appropriate than a single function. If the concept of the *ex ante* region is to become acceptable, it is essential to establish the boundaries that envelop it.

For simplicity, it is possible to think of an industry made up of a large number of competing firms, all producing identical outputs and, hence, based on the same technological information, but experiencing a wide variety of factor-price ratios. [4] We might, for example, rationalise this as the case of a large number of firms distributed among regions, each region with its own factor market, but producing for a single, highly competitive market. It is assumed further that the capital stock of each firm is made up of a mixture of vintages and that each firm invests in a new vintage in each subsequent period. For convenience, a period is defined such that an investment decision made during period $t-1$ will become operative during period $t$.

The inefficient boundary of the region, denoted $Y^0$, may be thought of as the locus of points drawn through the most efficient technologies already in use within the firms. Rationality appears to demand that we assume that firms do not choose a technology that is inferior to the best that they are currently using. In this case, the inefficient or best-practice boundary of period $t$ reflects the choices made from the *ex ante* region during period $t-1$. If the *ex ante* function of period $t-1$ had classical properties, then, given a sufficient spread of observations, the same would apply to the best-practice function of period $t$.

The efficient boundary defined here is a more theoretical construct. [5] Its existence stems from *a priori* beliefs about the relationship between the magnitude of R & D effort, changes in factor productivity, and changes in factor intensity. A simple R & D model will be developed in an attempt to isolate this boundary and it will become apparent during the analysis that it is this model that underlies the

Nordhaus concept (see Nordhaus, 1973) of the cost-isotech (or C-isotech) family. It is the C-isotech family that provides the essential link between the theories of innovation and production. It seems worth adding that Johansen (1972, p. 9) recognised that a more detailed consideration of the concept of the *ex ante* function would provide an opening to link the theory of production with innovation and the diffusion of new technologies.

For the remainder of this chapter, however, it is intended to use a different terminology. Nordhaus (1973, p. 211) defines the C-isotech in the following way: 'Ignoring uncertainty temporarily, we call the set of techniques attainable with a given cost C the C-isotech.' However, it is misnaming this line to call it the 'C-isotech'. It is the level of costs that is constant, and not the technology; and thus it seems more appropriate to call the line the 'technology-isocost' (or 'T-isocost') line.

To illustrate fully the relationship between R & D inputs and outputs, a single

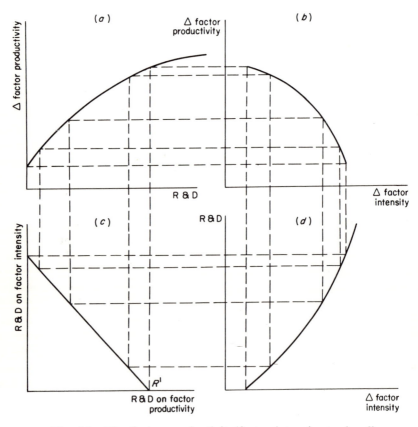

Fig. 4.1   The factor-productivity/factor-intensity trade-off

diagram of three dimensions is required. However, the analysis is simplified by setting out the various dimensions of the R & D model in separate, but related, diagrams. The model is shown in Figure 4.1. It concerns the nature of the innovations that can be produced by a single firm at a given time. [6] Two important characteristics of the innovations are considered in detail: changes in factor productivity and changes in factor intensity.

Figure 4.1(a) considers the relationship between R & D effort and the change in factor productivity that a given firm can achieve within the period. The existence of a limiting value of change in factor productivity may result from two constraints on the system.

1   The technology must be conceived of and developed ready for use in the production process between the times $t-1$ and $t$. Although technological potential may be boundless in the long run, in the short run it is almost certainly fixed. The shape of the curve stems from a belief that the more readily available and productive ideas will be used first, leaving the less productive ideas until higher levels of R & D intensity are reached.

2   At a given time there are limited resources that have a positive marginal product in R & D activities. This will act as a limiting factor on the size of the productivity change that can be achieved. The shape of the curve stems from the belief that at lower levels of R & D effort the most efficient resources will be used first, leaving the less efficient to be introduced at higher levels of effort.

A similar sort of relationship can be imagined to exist between R & D effort and the change in factor intensity that the firm can achieve. This relationship is shown in Figure 4.1(d). The underlying idea is that firms develop a stock of information and knowledge about the production process at the level (or levels) of factor intensity that they have experienced. Movement away from existing factor intensities will demand R & D effort. The greater the desired change, the greater will be the necessary effort. In addition, the argument about limited R & D resources and their quality is again pertinent in the short run.

It is Figure 4.1(c) that provides the essential link with the concept of the T-isocost line. Lines shown in this diagram describe given levels of R & D effort or cost, and this constant cost idea is an essential element of the Nordhaus concept. For any given level of R & D effort (for example, the level $R^1$), changes in productivity and factor intensity both compete for scarce resources, and the diagram illustrates the alternative allocations that can be made to either or both ends from a fixed R & D budget.

Given these three curves – i.e. those shown in Figure 4.1 parts (a), (c) and (d) – the trade-off between changes in productivity and factor intensity can be constructed directly. This trade-off curve is traced in Figure 4.1(b). Given invariant R & D production curves in parts (a) and (d) of the figure, different levels of R & D effort will produce alternative trade-off curves. Higher levels of effort will tend to shift it to the north-east, lower levels to the south-west. The outer boundary of the change in productivity and factor intensity trade-off curve corresponds to the maximum feasible R & D expenditure by the firm, $R^\infty$. However, it may also correspond to lower R & D levels if the marginal productivities of R & D inputs reach zero before $R$ reaches $R^\infty$.

The maximum R & D expenditure, $R^\infty$, does not have an obvious magnitude. In the extreme case we might consider it to be determined either by the potential supply of R & D inputs or by the fact that the marginal products of R & D inputs have become zero. Alternatively, it might be established according to economic criteria. It could, for example, be considered the expenditure necessary to carry out all R & D projects that are associated with a sum of discounted benefits that exceed the sum of discounted costs of R & D. But, so long as an upper bound to R & D can be envisaged for each firm in the industry, the question of its exact magnitude can be left open.

When drawn in the isoquant space of Figure 4.2, the trade-off curves for each firm from Figure 4.1(b) (one curve for each level of R & D expenditure) can be recognised as the T-isocost families described by Nordhaus. For simplicity, Figure 4.2 shows only the existing technology, $Y^0$, and the set of maximum achievable technologies, $X_j^\infty$, for each firm. The construction of $X_j^\infty$ from the trade-off

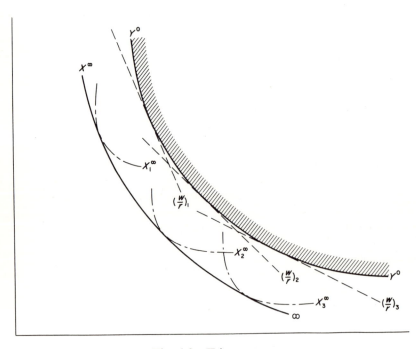

Fig. 4.2   T-isocost curves

48

curve in Figure 4.1(b) is described below. The ray through the existing best-practice point for each firm is drawn in Figure 4.2, and each ray corresponds to zero change in factor intensity for the associated firm. The size of productivity advance associated with this zero level of change in factor intensity from Figure 4.1(b) is then plotted along the ray for the appropriate firm in Figure 4.2. Other rays can be drawn around the original rays, and these correspond to greater changes in factor intensity. The corresponding levels of productivity advance from Figure 4.1(b) are measured along their length towards the origin. The resulting locus of points for the $j$th firm is represented by $X_j^\infty$. Each of these curves must be asymptotic to both a vertical and a horizontal line, because all technologies to the north-east of each point on such a curve can be achieved simply by hoarding one or both inputs.

This appears to be an appropriate point to define the remaining notation used in the chapter. The T-zero-isocost is denoted by $X_j^0(t)$, and it is represented by the line that joins the points in the isoquant space that are the most efficient available to the $j$th firm at time $t$ at zero R & D cost. The other members of the same family are denoted by $X_j^1(t), \ldots, X_j^\infty(t)$, in order of increasing magnitude of R & D effort (i.e. $R^1, \ldots, R^\infty$). Finally, the efficient industry boundary is defined as the envelope of all the individual firm boundaries, $X^\infty(t)$. Figure 4.2 describes a well-behaved case for both individual firm and industry curves.

### Costs of movement within the ex ante region: the role of the T-isocost family

Nordhaus (1973, p. 211) has stated that, 'The conventional production function is the C-zero-isotech.' In so far as the production function is a single point in the input–output space (i.e. the corner point of a right-angled isoquant arising from a Leontief production function), this seems plausible. Once the firm has experience of the technique represented by this point, it seems reasonable to assume that it could set up additional production units with identical characteristics without incurring further R & D costs. It is this form of production function that Nordhaus himself adopts and that is used here.

As a brief digression, however, it is interesting to consider a less restrictive production function. In the case of a classically shaped function, there is no inherent reason why the conventional production function should be the T-zero-isocost line, but if movements around the isoquant of such a function were entirely cost free, the T-isocost lines and the isoquants must coincide with one another. This gives rise to the special case of the isotechnology-isocost line. Nevertheless, it seems reasonable to assume that movements around the isoquant are, in practice, not cost free. Changes in factor intensity by the firm may at least require modifications to existing machines and augmentation of labour skills. [7] The T-isocost concept can be used to describe the costs of modifications that enable the firm to stay on the same isoquant. [8]

In the light of this discussion, it is interesting to reconsider the nature of the region's best-practice boundary. Because we have assumed that each firm possesses at least one unit of the latest vintage of capital, it is likely that the best-practice technique for each firm lies on or outside the industry's T-zero-isocost, $X^0(t)$. We have already noted the suggestion by Nordhaus that the conventional production function is the T-zero-isocost, but this will not be the case when, for example, some changes in factor productivity and intensity can be achieved without R & D cost (i.e. 'manna from heaven' or from 'learning by doing'). This possibly is reflected by positive intercepts on the factor-productivity and factor-intensity axes of parts (a) and (d) of Figure 4.1. When these functions pass through their respective origins, the best-practice function and the T-zero-isocost will coincide in at least one point. For simplicity it is assumed that this is the case.

Johansen (1972, p. 196) adopts the idea of a competitive industry composed of a large number of atomistic firms, but he recognises that it is unlikely that all of the points on the *ex ante* isoquants will be used. Nevertheless, Johansen claims that it is possible to imagine that these unobservable points do potentially exist and, indeed, would have been observed had slightly different factor–price ratios existed. The fact that the points do not exist in practice is explained by Salter (1966, p. 14): 'No engineer goes to the trouble and expense of developing techniques which he is certain will prove uneconomic.' This is in keeping with Johansen's belief (1972, p. 9) that the intermediate points could have been developed with a certain amount of R & D effort. It is, therefore, also consistent with the T-isocost concept.

If we draw in the firms' T-zero-isocost lines with the industry best-practice frontier they appear as in Figure 4.3. Certain assumptions underlie the two types of function drawn: first, that the best-practice function, $Y^0$, has classical properties;

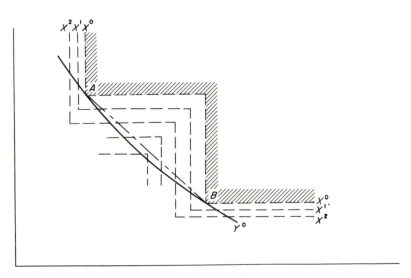

Fig 4.3   The T-isocost map where not all technologies are developed

second, that firms ($F_A$ and $F_B$) can always adopt technologies that lie inside their best-practice Leontief isoquant, without incurring positive R & D costs; and, third, that all technical changes are R & D induced.

Certain alternative inefficient boundary functions can now be visualised.

1   If production units are indivisible but all firms have complete knowledge of their competitors' technologies then the 'true' boundary is the line $X^0$ in Figure 4.3. If firms are unwilling to do any R & D but their factor-price ratio is changing, then their choices of technology are limited to their own T-zero-isocost until a competitor's technology becomes superior.

This is a rather interesting result. The T-isocost family is drawn and labelled $X^0$, $X^1$, $X^2$, ..., in Figure 4.3. The industry best-practice frontier, $Y^0$, is again sketched in. The curves indicate that if $F_A$ desires to move around the best-practice function starting from a point $A$, the costs of doing so increase with the size of the change: $R^0$, $R^1$, $R^2$, ... ; and then decrease: ..., $R^2$, $R^1$, $R^0$. This appears to be a useful way of capturing the notion that movements around the production function are not cost-free, although, in practice, the costs are unlikely to be simply those of R & D.

The explanation of the U-shaped cost curve is that $F_A$ will have less and less relevant experience the further it moves from its own factor intensity. On the other hand, its knowledge about its rivals' technologies will become more and more useful the closer the technology that $F_A$ desires to adopt is to that of a competitor. Alternatively, we might rationalise the U-shaped cost curve in terms of a single firm (for example, a capital-goods supplier) supplying new technologies to all firms in the industry. Such a firm would have experience of producing technologies for existing factor intensities, but not for intermediate intensities.

2   An alternative boundary results from assuming divisibility of production units in addition to perfect knowledge about competitors' technologies. In this case, linear programming theory indicates that the technologies of $F_A$ and $F_B$ can be combined in various proportions. The T-zero-isocost is now formed by the straight line $AB$ in Figure 4.3, and hence approximates the best-practice isoquant, $Y^0$, much more closely.

3   In the extreme case of no knowledge about rivals' technologies there is no single boundary to the *ex ante* region. There is, however, a boundary associated with each individual firm: $X_1^0, X_2^0, X_3^0, \ldots$. In this case, perfect divisibility of production units has no impact on the nature of the boundary. Cost-free combinations of $F_A$'s and $F_B$'s technologies are not possible, because $F_B$'s technology is unknown to $F_A$.

*A digression on the possibility of technical regress*

If we adopt the firm as the basic decision-making unit and assume that its *ex ante* possibilities and their costs are summarised by its T-isocost family, then it can be shown that, under conditions of changing factor-price ratios with low levels of

c

R & D effort, technical regress may occur. In the sense used here, technical regress means that the industry best-practice isoquant moves outwards and firms in the industry adopt equipment that is technically inferior to the existing best-practice for the industry as a whole.

Figure 4.4 gives the essence of the argument. $Y^0(1)$ summarises the industry best-practice boundary at time 1. It is a theoretical construct in that it is the envelope of all the best-practice techniques used by the various firms in the industry. For

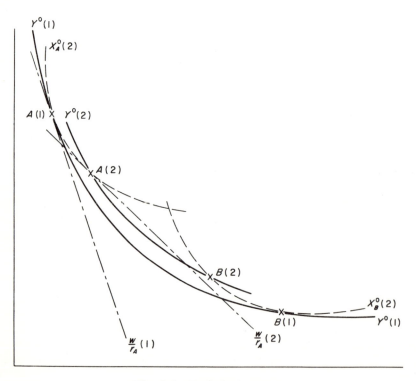

Fig. 4.4   Technical regress

simplicity we again assume that each firm has at least one production unit that lies on this evelope. It is also assumed that each firm could invest in an identical unit in subsequent periods without incurring positive R & D costs. In other words, the T-zero-isocost of period 2, $X_j^0(2)$, is assumed to touch the isoquant $Y^0(1)$ as shown in the diagram. The remaining T-isocost lines in the family do exist but, for the sake of simplicity, are not drawn.

Consider $F_A$ at time 1. Its perception of the *ex ante* alternatives are summarised not by the industry-level best-practice isoquant, but by the T-isocost family it faces and, more particularly, by the single T-isocost line that is left once the decision about the level of R & D effort has been taken. Suppose that this firm chooses to invest in a production unit characterised by the point $A(1)$, where the wage–rental ratio $w/r_A(1)$ is a tangent to the corresponding industry- and firm-level *ex ante* isoquants. Having experienced technology $A(1)$, the T-zero-isocost line for the firm moves inwards, so that by period 2 it is represented by $X_A^0(2)$.

If, during period 2, $F_A$ decides that it is not going to spend any money at all on R & D, then, under conditions of zero knowledge about competitors' technologies, its *ex ante* possibilities are summarised by $X_A^0(2)$. A new wage–rental ratio, $w/r_A(2)$, will induce the firm to invest in a technology characterised by the point $A(2)$. Other firms may also experience movements in their factor costs, while economic conditions may constrain them to make similar decisions about their level of R & D effort during the period. Thus, for example, $F_B$ may decide to invest in a technique represented in Figure 4.4 by the point $B(2)$. If we suppose, for the sake of argument, that all such points lie on the same industry isoquant, $Y^0(2)$, then this isoquant is inferior to the best-practice function established in period 1. Cases can be envisaged where higher levels of R & D effort will still result in this rather restricted form of technical regress.

Under perfect knowledge about competitors' technologies, but where production units are indivisible, firms may be able to remain on the existing best-practice boundary or at least to move closer to it than in the previous case. In this case, the trochoidal curve formed by $X_A^0(2)$ up to the point where it cuts $X_B^0(2)$, and thereafter by the second curve, summarises the *ex ante* possibilities. Where the new wage–rental ratio, $w/r_A(1)$, cuts through a competitor's T-zero-isocost, the case is identical to that described previously. But, if the segment of the best-practice function cut off by $w/r_A(2)$ contains part of a competitor's T-zero-isocost, it then becomes optimal for $F_A$ to adopt a technology from $F_B$'s family.

Where there exists perfect knowledge of competitor's technologies and perfect divisibility of production units, then, given a sufficiently large number of competitors distributed fairly evenly in the isoquant space, the line $Y^0(1)$ closely approximates the *ex ante* alternatives and the possibility of technical regress is greatly reduced.

The final outcome depends on the exact nature of the real world. If the real world is ill informed and production units tend to be indivisible, there is very real danger of technical regress at the intensive margin where factor-price ratios are changing but firms are unwilling to carry out R & D. The better informed firms are, and the more divisible the additional production units, the lower are the chances of experiencing this form of regress. It is worth adding, however, that it is quite another thing to suggest that technical regress at the intensive margin could result in a reduction in the average overall productivity of factors.

### The 'effective' ex ante isoquant

Acceptance of the concept of the *ex ante* region implies that the *ex ante* functions that typically characterise putty–clay production functions and growth models are invalid. The only exception is where the points chosen from the *ex ante* region lie on a classically shaped function in the input–output space (i.e. the 'effective' *ex ante* function has classical properties). Is it possible that market conditions and forces could constrain the choices of entrepreneurs in this way? It is argued below that the conditions that Johansen (1972, pp. 13–19) imposes on the simplest 'short-run macro function' may, when applied to the *ex ante* function, go a long way towards ensuring that the latter has the desired classical properties.

The approach adopted in this chapter has a great deal in common with Samuelson's construction of the surrogate production function (see Samuelson, 1962). Samuelson imagined there to be an economy composed of a large number of production units, each characterised by a fixed-coefficient production function. Perfect information in the capital and labour markets in conjunction with perfect competition in the final product markets were the key elements in ensuring that technologies that were inefficient (i.e. those whose total factor rewards were dominated by at least one other technology) were automatically eliminated from production. The envelope of efficient technologies was a curve possessing the following properties: 'constant returns to scale . . . smooth substitutability and well-behaved marginal-productivity partial derivatives'. Thus, if only efficient points from the fixed-coefficient world are utilised, they appear to have been drawn from a function possessing classical properties.

For the purposes of this chapter, a slightly different – and, in certain respects, more realistic – view of the world is adopted. The discussion is restricted to a single industry. The firms that compose the industry produce a single product and perfect competition exists in the final product market. Firms are assumed to establish individual production units, each of which must be economically viable in its own right. These units are distributed among the various regions of the country. Factor rewards may differ between regions in such a way that, at any given time, a wide variety of factor-price ratios can exist. To simplify the model, however, the supplies of the various factors within each region are assumed to be highly elastic. It will become apparent during the attempt to isolate the 'effective' *ex ante* function that the model adopted stresses the cost reducing aspects of competition. [9]

To establish the possible existence of a single 'effective' *ex ante* function possessing classical properties, a rather limited, although not wholly unrealistic, model of the firm is adopted. Each firm is capable of carrying out R & D on behalf of the production unit that it plans to establish. The costs of R & D can be thought of as entrepreneurial disutility, because of the associated effort and loss of leisure time. Here it is suggested that entrepreneurial utility, $EU$ is a function of the profitability of the firm, $\pi$, and the level of entrepreneurial effort, $EE$:

$$EU = U(\pi, EE)$$

Because the industry is expected to remain highly competitive, firms will only earn normal profits, $\pi^{\min}$, which are defined as those necessary just to induce firms to invest in new production units. Entrepreneurs can now be considered to minimise effort, subject to earning normal profits:

minimise $\quad EE$

subject to $\quad \pi = \pi^{\min}$

An alternative and perhaps more appealing rationalisation of the model can be found in the theory of 'managerial capitalism'. As Marris (1971) points out, this is closely linked with the separation of ownership from control and with the disappearance of the classical entrepreneur. It is, for example, by no means certain that the aspirations of members of an R & D department and those of firm management will be in accord. As Steele (1969, p. 147) points out, this conflict of goals may be very real, placing R & D management in an uncomfortable position: 'What he [the R & D manager] must learn to do is establish and maintain a viable accommodation between the needs and aspirations of his research people on the one hand, and the demands of his sponsoring organisation on the other.' The minimum it appears possible for the R & D team to achieve – without alienating firm management and risking redundancy – is to comply with management directions to solve the problems associated with keeping the firm competitive. Having satisfied this need, the group may then return to its own goals. Thus, the analysis is closely aligned with the concept of 'satisficing' behaviour developed in Simon (1959).

Under the conditions set out above, we should be able to say something about the nature of the 'effective' *ex ante* function. One thing is certain: this function must have special properties that allow it to reconcile a variety of factor-price ratios with the existence of a perfectly competitive product market. Consider firms $F_A$, $F_B$ and $F_C$ with their respective price lines $P_A$, $P_B$ and $P_C$, where $P_A > P_B$ and $P_B = P_C$. This is the situation shown in Figure 4.5. The price lines have the property that, the further they are from the origin, the higher the price they represent. $P_A$, for example, is a higher price line than $P_A^*$. But a problem arises when we try to compare lines of different slopes. However, it is fairly obvious that $P_A$ is inferior not only to $P_A^*$, but also to $P_B$ and $P_C$. In addition, while we cannot say that $P_A^*$ is (or is not) directly inferior to $P_B$, it is inferior to $P_C$ (and hence to $P_B$). We might then imagine other price lines less steep than $P_B$ and $P_C$, although steeper than $P_A$, but representing a price level equal to that of $P_B$ and $P_C$. Such lines will force $P_A$ down to a position such as $P_A^{**}$, where $P_A^{**} = P_B = P_C$. Given a sufficiently large number of alternative factor-price ratios, a construct analogous to Samuelson's (1962, diagram 2) is obtained.

It seems intuitively plausible that it is the envelope of these prices lines, $Y^e$, that is the classical function being sought. The curve $Y^e$ has the property that each price line is a tangent to it; and, hence, the slope of the function at any given point is the same as the wage–rental ratio at that point. It is as if firms choose from the 'effective' *ex ante* function, paying the factors employed the marginal products they earn. If we assume, for simplicity, that normal profits are zero, then the whole

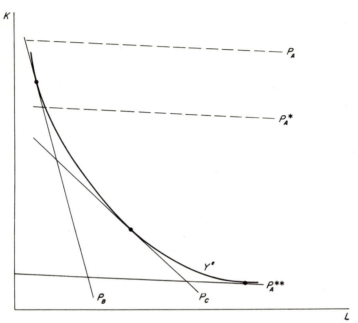

Fig. 4.5    Derivation of the 'effective' *ex ante* function

of the product is distributed between capital and labour according to Euler's theorem; and Allen (1969, pp. 433–4) has already shown that any linear homogenous function

$$Y = L\phi\left(\frac{K}{L}\right)$$

satisfies this property.

Despite the fact that we have isolated the function that intuition may suggest is the 'effective' *ex ante* function, we have not analysed how the firm moves to its final investment option. Indeed, it will become apparent that, while the function we have been examining may be an approximation to the 'effective' *ex ante* function, in practice firms may choose points some distance away from it. Figure 4.6 considers the case of $F_A$, whose original choice of technology was $A$ on the T-isocost line $X_A^0$. This choice minimises its R & D, but the associated price line $P_A$ exceeds the competitive norm, and a plant established with this technology will fail to yield

56

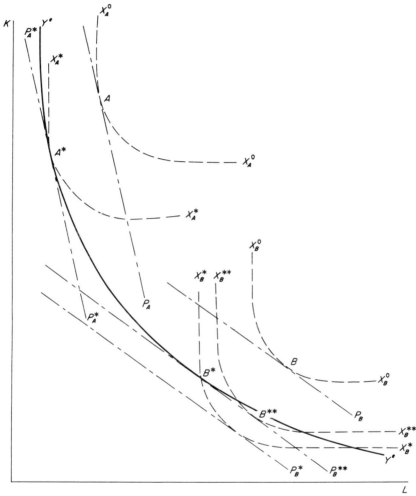

Fig. 4.6 The 'effective' *ex ante* function: a badly behaved case

normal profits (i.e. it does not satisfy the constraint that $\pi \geqq \pi^{\min}$). The optimal position is associated with a level of research $R^*$, which enables $F_A$ to reach $A^*$ on $X_A^*$. The associated price line, $P_A^*$, is at the competitive norm and the firm earns normal profits. In the diagram, $P_A^*$ is shown to be a tangent to both $Y^e$ and $Y_A^*$. The case of $F_B$ is slightly different. The point of tangency between $Y^e$ and $P_B^{**}$ is considered suboptimal by the firm. Given the shape of the T-isocost line $X_B^*$, the firm can reach a still lower unit cost line, $P_B^*$, without any additional research effort.

But the R & D minimising behaviour of firms will induce $F_B$ to make $B^{**}$ its final investment option. In so doing, its price per unit of output is identical to its rivals', but its choice of technology lies inside the expected 'effective' *ex ante* function $Y^e$. The problem is that the set of points $K, L$ consistent with a given price regime $P^0, w, r$ are given by $Y = f(K, L)$. So too are the equilibrium points between the T-isocost map and the price lines. Only by chance, or if the T-isocost map and the isoquants

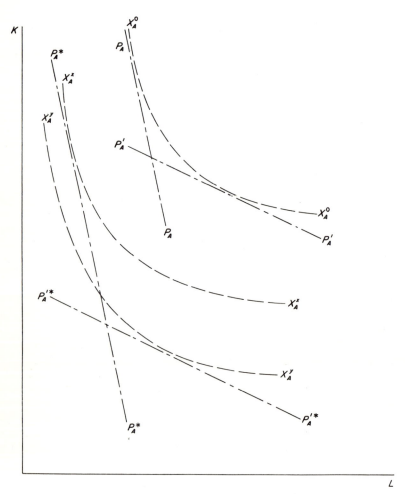

Fig. 4.7   Factor prices, location and the size of the R & D effort

are identically shaped, will the profit-maximising R & D result in a point on the appropriate 'effective' *ex ante* function.

In general, the closer the factor intensity of the original investment option to that of the final option, the smaller will be the R & D effort demanded of the firm. Figure 4.7 enables this point to be considered in more detail. The diagram shows $F_A$'s technology to have become inappropriate in the light of the factor-price ratio in the region where its production has traditionally taken place. The slope of the price line $P'_A$ denotes the wage–rental ratio, and $X^0_A$, $X^x_A$ and $X^y_A$ denote three T-isocost lines drawn from $F_A$'s family of T-isocosts. With this factor-price ratio, $F_A$ must make an effort $R^y$ to reach $X^y_A$, which enables it to charge the competitive norm $P'^*_A$ for its product. It is, however, fairly obvious that the firm's technical knowledge is more appropriate to certain other regions – for example, the one characterised by $P_A$. In this case, to reach the price norm, $P^*_A$, the firm needs an effort of only $R^x$, where $R^x < R^y$.

If we suppose that $R^x$ is the largest R & D effort $F_A$ can make (i.e. $R^x = R^\infty$), then $F_A$ will be forced to change regions if it insists on setting up a new plant. Presumably, if it is an R & D minimiser, it will move to a region that enables it to attain the competitive price norm with the least effort. An analysis of this kind obviously can provide some insights about the changing distribution of firms between regions and even countries.

## Conclusions

This chapter emphasises the fact that the *ex ante* concept requires greater theoretical rigour and that the idea of an *ex ante* region is intuitively more appealing. There is always the possibility that points chosen from such a region may appear 'as if' they are drawn from a well-behaved *ex ante* function. While the concept of a T-isocost map provides one method of comparing different points from the region, the likelihood that the points chosen from the region having the appearance of a well-behaved function is extremely remote. Cost-minimising behaviour with respect to the R & D decision is unlikely to lead to firms establishing points on a unique *ex ante* function.

The analysis developed in this chapter assumes that all new production units are in competition with one another. In this way, the nature of the existing set of units owned by firms can be ignored. In practice, the past experience of firms and the characteristics of their existing technologies are likely to play a crucial role in deciding the nature of the new technologies drawn from the *ex ante* alternatives. The less competitive the firm, given its existing technology, the more radical its activity at the intensive margin must be in order to restore it to a competitive position. Firms that go against this rule will tend to disappear from the productive system. The implication is that firms will tend to subserviate their R & D activities to finding solutions to their overall competitive position, and this may involve a search procedure of the behavioural type. However, a wide variety of existing technologies and efficiencies means an even greater diversity of technologies adopted at the intensive margin, and makes the well-behaved *ex ante* function an even more remote outcome.


**Notes**

[1] Of the type described by Allen (1968, p. 44) and Brown (1966, pp. 29–31).

[2] See, for example, the work of Kaldor (1957), Phelps (1966) and Conlisk (1973).

[3] See, for example, Machlup (1962), Schmookler (1966), Nordhaus (1969) and Kamien and Schwartz (1972).

[4] For a more detailed discussion of the reasons that underlie this choice see Johansen (1972, p. 196). Basically, it ensures that we are looking at a single family of isoquants and that we can see their full shape.

[5] It has certain parallels with the inner boundary between the regions of structural and frictional unemployment outlined by Lipsey (1965).

[6] Exactly the same arguments can be applied to a capital-goods producer considering his activities for each individual firm he supplies.

[7] Svennilson (1964, p. 158) gives a brief discussion about some of the alternative forms of modification.

[8] It is worth noting, as Fellner (1973, pp. 158–9) points out, that such types of modification may, in fact, also change the nature and position of the isoquant without changing the technique of production.

[9] See Williams (1967, pp. 71–2).

# 5 The ex ante function and the ex post micro function

## Introduction

Economists have become increasingly aware that problems of aggregation can result in the failure of aggregate production functions to reflect the underlying technology of production. Such fears give micro studies much of their appeal. At a very low level of aggregation, extraneous influences should be less important and estimates should directly reflect the micro technologies. Despite the potential insights about the technology of production that research at this level promises to yield, few studies of production have worked at such a detailed level. There are two main causes of this lack of interest: first, there are severely restrictive data constraints at the micro level; and, second, the good empirical performance of aggregate functions has detracted from the incentive to carry out more detailed studies.

Here we investigate the nature of the micro production relationships that form the building blocks from which more aggregate vintage models are constructed. This chapter attempts to demonstrate that a putty–clay model of the traditional type can be derived directly from these building blocks. The emphasis is on deriving a function that can be estimated, and particular attention is paid to the nature of the function under different *ex ante* regimes and to the importance of capacity usage. This route to obtaining an aggregate function is followed because the UK data are inadequate to enable each micro function to be estimated individually. Given some ingenuity, a more aggregate putty–clay relationship can be estimated on the basis of published UK data, and the results of this provide insights about the underlying micro technologies.

## Recent empirical work relevant to engineering

There are a number of micro studies relevant to the theme of this chapter that are in general accord with the concept of an integrated production schema. A number of these are discussed in some detail by Johansen (1972, chapter 8). This section very briefly reviews the much smaller number that draw their evidence from the engineering industries.

An important study by Kurz and Manne (1963) considered the substitution possibilities between various types of metal-cutting machine tools, drawing on the extremely detailed data constructed by Markowitz and Rowe (1961). The observations recorded were of output and investment per head associated with each production unit capable of executing a certain group of tasks. Each observation corresponds in principle to an *ex post* micro function. Kurz and Manne claimed that a number of the possibilities would be used by firms only in an emergency, and under normal circumstances would be uneconomic. For this reason they devised a system for deleting supposedly inefficient possibilities – omitting those for which investment per head was greater, but output no higher, than for other units. This censoring rule has been severely criticised by Furubotn (1965), Lave (1966) and Johansen (1972, pp. 191–5). One major criticism was that a higher investment cost may reflect a more durable piece of equipment that, in comparison to its less durable counterparts, is incapable of a greater output in the short run, but is capable of a far greater output in the long run.

Johansen (1972, pp. 191 and 193) claims that the production function fitted to these remaining observations is close to reflecting the *ex ante* function, and that it would have been even closer had Kurz and Manne fitted a frontier function. However, in so far as the points reflect equipment already in use, the fitted relationship appears to be the best-practice function (or a 'dated' *ex ante* function) rather than a summary of the current *ex ante* choices. Information about the capacity established within the firm, with technical characteristics $\xi^1, \xi^2$ – i.e $f(\xi^1, \xi^2)$ – is not given in the Kurz and Manne study, and as a result the data are not sufficient to construct the short-run macro function.

Capital and labour usage were the subject of a study by Dudley et al. (1968). This study looked at the periods of idleness of both men and machines within different sections (i.e. different shops, such as machine, press and assembly shops) of plants in four UK engineering industries. The aim was to estimate the potential productivity gains from eliminating underutilisation of factors. Idleness of this type is closely allied to Liebenstein's 'X-inefficiency' (see Liebenstein, 1966, 1969). Their estimates of the potential increases in productivity appeared to be based on the hypothesis of constant returns to working equipment and labour more intensely. The assumption of constant returns underlies the basic Johansen *ex post* micro function.

The works of Bell (1972) and Senker and Hugget (1973) were attempts to isolate the implications of technological change for the manpower requirements of the UK engineering industry. Their analysis was essentially qualitative, and they made little attempt to develop an integrated theoretical framework. However, their approach is broadly consistent with a vintage model. The main causal link that enables them to make predictions is shown in Figure 2.5 above. Senker et al. (1975, pp. 86–9) gave evidence that often one man operates a single piece of equipment or a set of installations, which suggests that patterns of capital–labour matching may be isolated by observing particular processes in different firms. This approach is adopted in the empirical work reported here.

Senker et al. (1975, p. 111) were, however, worried that 'inter-process links' make it difficult to trace the implications for manpower throughout the firm. While these secondary effects will be more difficult to assess than the primary effects (i.e. those associated with manning the new techniques), Senker et al. (1975, p. 114) were also worried that protracted adjustment to new techniques where there is some choice in the way adjustment occurs may make it necessary to 'Abandon . . . the assumption that there is a relatively fixed and technically determined relationship between a technique and its associated labour force.' Rather than dismiss primary relationships out of hand, however, it seems sensible to test for their existence empirically where data exist.

## Data availability at the micro level

At the level of individual processes or tasks it is extremely difficult to obtain the compatible data essential in the estimation of production relationships. In order to emphasise the problems posed for this study by data constraints, consideration is given to each of the different kinds of information.

### Output data

One of the most important problems faced in an empirical study of the putty–clay model is associated with the lack of comprehensive output data at this level of detail. The measure of output required obviously depends on the particular process that we are looking at and, for a given process, we still have to decide what that measure might be. What, for example, is the best measure of output for welding – the number of welds made? Even in this simple case the measure may not be adequate: welds may differ in size and strength. There is, anyway, no published source that records the number of welds carried out by particular firms or industries.

There are two possible ways of avoiding the measurement-of-output problem. The first is to assume that the output of each process enters the final product in a fixed proportion,

$$Y_x = a_x Y \tag{5.1}$$

where $x$ denotes the $x$th process and $a$ is a constant. Hence, if

$$Y_x = f_x(K_x, L_x) \tag{5.2}$$

represents the production relationship relevant for the $x$th process, the production function that can be estimated is

$$Y = \frac{1}{a_x} f_x(K_x, L_x) \tag{5.3}$$

The second method is to assume that entrepreneurs adjust the ratio of factor inputs in a cost-minimising way. This transforms the production function, equation (5.2), into employment function form:

$$L_x = g_x(K_x, w_x, r_x) \tag{5.4}$$

The theoretical analysis uses this last assumption in order to derive a functional form that can be estimated given current data supplies.

*Capital stock*

Historically, many studies have found great difficulty in obtaining useful information about the stock of capital available for use in production. There are, however, quite detailed estimates available for the engineering industries' stocks of different types of machine tools in 1961, 1966 and 1971. The *Census of Metal Working Machine Tools* appears quinquennially and reports estimates of the numbers of machines, categorised by type, industry and age, [1] in the engineering industries. The importance of the data cannot be doubted. In a study that attempted to provide estimates of the stock of capital, Pyatt (1964b, pp. 24–5) stated that, 'Thought of in physical terms, gross investment is simply the number of buildings, machinery and vehicles purchased in a year. Thus, ideally, data on physical gross investment should take the form of a list of assets. These lists, however, would have to be so numerous and so detailed that compiling them on a national scale would be impossible.' The information given in the *Census of Metal Working Machine Tools* is used in this chapter to consider directly the manning requirements (i.e. men–machine ratios) for various tasks.

The data are not comprehensive, and the coverage of capital types leaves much to be desired. Metalworking machine tools (particularly cutting and forming tools) are considered in some detail, but other types of machinery are given little or no coverage (though, partly because of the advent of new machine types, there is more detail in the more recent censuses). On the other hand, the list of industries covered enables a minimum of eighteen MLHs (or groups of MLHs) to be distinguished in all census years. By 1971, most of the relevant engineering industries were separately covered.

*Labour data*

Since 1963 the Engineering Industry Training Board (EITB), in conjunction with the Department of Employment, has collected employment data, categorised by skill, sex and industry, for the engineering industries. This MLH-level data has been released by the EITB at a level of skill aggregation much higher than that at which it was collected. The Department of Employment on the other hand, has published in its *Gazette* a very detailed breakdown of skills, but only for fairly broad industry groups (eight engineering groups). With the exception of one or two skill categories (for instance, welding and metal fabricating) the published information is not sufficiently detailed to be useful in a study of the kind undertaken in this chapter. The EITB was kind enough to release for this study information relating to the small number of skills that can be appropriately matched with machine types.

*Shiftworking*

One variable that has received little attention in the literature on production and employment functions is shiftworking. It is possible for a given piece of equipment to be worked at greatly different intensities depending on the shift system in operation. A given unit of capital may have an average working day of eight hours in a firm that does not use shiftworking or overtime, while in a firm operating a continuous three eight-hour shift system the same machine could be in use (excluding maintenance and repair) for 24 hours a day. This study uses data from the *Ministry of Labour Gazette* (1965) and the *New Earnings Survey* (1970).

A major reason why economists have tended to neglect this aspect of the technology of production is the lack of published information. Until recently, the only information was found in two spot observations, relating to 1954 and 1964, published in the *Ministry of Labour Gazette* (1954, 1965). This source gives detailed MLH information about the nature and prevalence of various shiftworking systems. The *New Earnings Survey* is the source of data for 1968 and later years. It does not record detailed information about the prevalence of various shiftworking systems, but gives information about shiftworking premia payments. The report of the National Board for Prices and Incomes (1970, vol. 2, p. 118) argues that shift premia data are deficient in so far as people working the normal shift of a shift system are not paid premia. The report notes that, 'The effect of this wider definition is that in manufacturing, for example, 25 per cent of adult manual workers are classified as shiftworkers though only 21 per cent had shift premia.'

*Capital usage*

A study of a vintage formulation requires data about capital usage. This chapter concentrates on machine tools and, following Heathfield (1972a), electricity-consumption data are assumed to reflect plant and machinery usage. The usage series were calculated from the fuel-consumption data used in various other parts of the study and constructed as described in detail in Appendix II. The method is the same as that adopted by Evans (1974), who attempted to estimate the degree of labour hoarding in the engineering industry. Time-series regressions are estimated for each MLH, such that

$$E = a + bt + u$$

where $E$ denotes electricity consumption, $t$ is a time trend and $u$ is an error term. The lines are then shifted parallel in an upwards direction (altering the value of $a$ to $a'$) to pass through the observed $E_t$ with the largest residual. This revision ensures that $u_t \leq 0$ for all $t$. The values $\hat{E}_t$ are then calculated such that

$$\hat{E} = a' + bt$$

and then the usage figures are given by

$$U_t = \frac{E_t}{\hat{E}_t}$$

*Wage data*

The most complicated of the functional forms require quite detailed information about the price of labour over a very long period. Two alternative measures of the price of labour are wage rates and earnings. If entrepreneurs, when making decisions involving wage information, assume that employees work normal hours and undertake no shiftworking, then wage rates appear to be the appropriate price variables. However, Wabe (1974, p. 28) has shown that over much of the post-war period average hours worked have consistently stayed above normal hours; and, in addition, the discussion of shiftworking indicated that it was an important and permanent aspect of the production technology. Hence, employers will generally build an element of overtime and shiftworking costs into their labour-price calculations. Thus, average earnings appear to be a better indicator of labour costs than a notional wage rate.

While increasingly detailed information is becoming available, it does not yet exist at a sufficiently high level of industry or skill disaggregation, or over a long-enough period. The information required to complement the 1971 machine-tool data relate to 'average' or 'typical' earnings in the three decades prior to 1971. The only published earnings data at an MLH level covering this period are found in the *Census of Production*. The censuses do not provide a continuous series and it was necessary to assume that the 1948, 1958 and 1968 earnings data were 'typical' of each of the three decades. The data used in this study relate to manual workers and exclude the white-collar occupations. The earnings data relate to all manual workers and not to particular skills such as turners, but they have to serve for the purposes of this study.

There are a number of problems with the data. One particular inconsistency is that the 1948 information refers to Great Britain, while the 1958 and 1968 data relate to the United Kingdom. The most difficult problem is to reconcile the changes in industrial classification that have taken place between 1948 and 1968. The 1963 census reports the 1958 information on a basis broadly compatible with the 1968 MLHs, but the 1948 information is reported by more aggregate industry groups and the classification is much more difficult to reconcile with the classifications used in later years. By going to the individual census reports, however, information is available about specialisations within each industry group (see table 6 of each report), and in many cases the subgroups reported match fairly closely the MLHs distinguished in later years. The data available in the 1948 census about subgroups related to total employment and the corresponding wage bill, and not just to manual workers. The manual-employment and wage data for the 1948 MLHs were subdivided according to the ratio of workers in each subgroup to total employment, and the ratio of the wage bill of the subgroup to the total MLH wage bill. Those parts of, or whole, 1948 MLHs that were not allocated to 1968 MLHs were put into the 'not elsewhere specified' groups (339, 349, 369, 389 or 399). In most cases, the resulting levels of employment, wage bills and earnings appeared to be realistic, but the results are tentative and should be treated with caution.

*Rental data*

The measurement of price per unit of capital raises problems even more difficult

66

than those associated with the labour input. The notion of a rental is adopted as the indicator of price that a firm might use in assessing its investment strategy, and it is defined as the amount a firm would have to pay if it hired a unit of capital for a year. Current rental data could be collected, but this would prove both difficult and time consuming. In addition, this study requires rental data over three decades. Only price information for machines is available over this period and this is far from ideal.

The initial step in constructing rentals for turning machines was to calculate quality-constant price indices over the period 1948–72. The approach is based on the hedonic procedure described in Bosworth (1976), where prices are regressed on average weight, $W$, cumulative patenting activity, $J$, and a time trend, $t$, for four subcategories of turning machines as well as for the turning group as a whole. [2] The patent term was allowed to lag or lead the dependent variable as there was no *a priori* information about when an invention would be used relative to the date at which it was patented. The log-linear regression

$$\log p = a + bt + c \log W + d \log J + u \tag{5.5}$$

gives the most acceptable results, and these are reported in Table 5.1.

The functions all have a high explanatory power and all the variables are significant at the 1 per cent level. A note of caution must be sounded, however, because the $DW$ statistic was significant at the 5 per cent level in three of the five cases. In this respect the results were inferior to those reported in the other study (Bosworth, 1976). The main cause was probably the inability to distinguish the $J$ variable appropriate to each machine type. Table 5.2 reports the quality-constant rates of inflation and compares them with the crude rate of price change based on a simple exponential time trend.

Quality-constant prices for the five machine categories were evaluated about their geometric mean sample values for the post-war period, and values for 1948, 1958 and 1968 were calculated for each of the machine types except the numerical-control category, which is a phenomenon of the last decade and for which only a 1968 price was calculated. The effect of holding quality constant is to raise prices in earlier years relative to later years. The price data were transformed into rentals by dividing them by the estimated life expectancies, $T$, of the various types of machines in the different industries. The $T$ variable was constructed using information from the *Census of Metal Working Machine Tools* using the approach advocated by Bacon and Eltis (1974). Where centre lathes are studied in the empirical section, the rentals from the 'other lathes' category are used (because centre lathes are by far the largest component of this group). In the case where 'all lathes' are being studied, the rental is constructed as a weighted average of the four types of lathes, where the weights applied are based on the proportions of the various types held by each MLH.

Table 5.1

Hedonic results for turning machines[a]

| Regression | Machine type | Period of $J$ | $a$ | $b$ | $c$ | $d$ | $\bar{R}^2$ | $F$ | $DW$ |
|---|---|---|---|---|---|---|---|---|---|
| (1) | All turning | $t+2$ | 2·3900** | 0·0331** | 1·0427** | 0·0920** | 0·969 | 239·51** | 2·0100 |
| (2) | Automatics | $t+1$ | 4·6392** | 0·0282** | 0·9775** | 0·2455** | 0·996 | 1942·63** | 1·7825 |
| (3) | Capstan and turret | $t+1$ | 5·4654** | 0·0376** | 0·6147** | 0·1382 | 0·960 | 169·30** | 1·0282** |
| (4) | Other lathes | $t+1$ | 4·3604** | 0·0258* | 0·6811** | 0·2207* | 0·965 | 196·54** | 0·8668** |
| (5) | Numerically controlled lathes | — | 6·4543** | 0·0629 | 0·8753* | — | 0·558 | 4·16 | 3·6291** |

[a] Levels of significance in this and subsequent tables are denoted by:

† significant at the 10% level
* significant at the 5% level
** significant at the 1% level.

Table 5.2

Post-war rates of price change for turning machines

| Regression | Machine type | Quality-constant rate of inflation | Crude rate of price change |
|---|---|---|---|
| (1) | All turning | 3·31 | 10·47 |
| (2) | Automatics | 2·82 | 10·82 |
| (3) | Capstan and turret | 3·76 | 5·45 |
| (4) | Other lathes | 2·58 | 4·90 |
| (5) | Numerically controlled | 6·29 | 8·34 |

**Ex ante choices and the nature of the ex post micro function**

The *ex ante* function plays a central role in determining the nature of the *ex post* micro functions. Imperfect knowledge of the *ex ante* relationship hinders the formulation of realistic *ex post* functions and, given the data constraints, only the simplest *ex ante* functions are adopted. By making a number of alternative assumptions about the nature of the *ex ante* function, the associated *ex post* micro functions can be derived. The particular cases of *ex ante* putty and clay are considered in detail below.

As data are available that should make a cross-sectional study feasible, the analysis is developed in terms of cross-sectional functional forms. It is argued that if we can observe a number of production units established at the same time (and hence on the basis of the same technology) but experiencing a variety of relative factor prices, then it should be possible to establish not only the *ex post* micro functions, but also the *ex ante* functions from which they were drawn. In the theoretical and empirical analysis that follows, we consider a single production process at a time. This enables us to simplify the notation by suppressing the $x$ subscript (relating to the $x$th production process).

*The* ex ante *clay case*

In this case it is assumed that there is no choice of new technologies. There exists, at each point in time, a single new technology that is the most efficient over the whole range of conceivable factor-price ratios. Assuming that there is a single labour skill and capital type used in each production process, the production function can be written

$$Y_{jv} - \frac{1}{\xi_v^K} K_{jv} = \frac{1}{\xi_v^L} L_{jv} \qquad (5.6)$$

where $j$ denotes the $j$th plant, $(j = 1, \ldots, m)$ and $v$ the $v$th vintage $(v = 1, \ldots, \tau,$ where $\tau$ is the oldest vintage in use). If output data are not available it can be made implicit in the following way:

$$L_{jv} = \frac{\xi_v^L}{\xi_v^K} K_{jv} = \psi_v K_{jv} \qquad (5.7)$$

69

*The* ex ante *putty case*

Traditionally, economic theory suggests that a variety of *ex ante* choices are possible. The choice of technology by the *j*th firm is now determined by the shape of the *ex ante* function, and, assuming cost-minimising entrepreneurial behaviour, the actual or expected factor-price ratio. We consider just two cases: the Cobb–Douglas function and the more general CES *ex ante* form.

*The Cobb–Douglas function.* The *ex ante* function relating to one such process can then be written

$$Y_{jv} = A_v K_{jv}^{\alpha_v} L_{jv}^{\beta_v} \tag{5.8}$$

where $A$ is the technical-efficiency parameter and the powers $\alpha$ and $\beta$ are production coefficients (which reflect capital's and labour's share in output). The associated cost function is

$$C_{jv} = r_{jv} K_{jv} + w_{jv} L_{jv}) \tag{5.9}$$

where $w$ is the wage rate and $r$ the rental, while $C$ denotes the total costs of operating the production unit. If management attempts to minimise costs, the choices of new technologies will be determined by considering the Lagrangian

$$LG = A_v K_{jv}^{\alpha_v} L_{jv}^{\beta_v} + \lambda(C_{jv} - r_{jv} K_{jv} - w_{jv} L_{jv}) \tag{5.10}$$

where $\lambda$ is the Lagrangian multiplier. From the marginal conditions, cost-minimising behaviour implies that

$$L_{jv} = \frac{\beta_v}{\alpha_v} \frac{r_{jv}}{w_{jv}} K_{jv} \tag{5.11}$$

*The general CES function.* If the Cobb–Douglas function is replaced by the more general CES form, equation (5.8) becomes

$$LG = \zeta_v (a_v K_{jv}^{-\Phi_v} + b_v L_{jv}^{-\Phi_v})^{-\theta_v/\Phi_v} + \lambda(C_{jv} - w_{jv} L_{jv} - r_{jv} K_{jv}) \tag{5.12}$$

The marginal conditions [3] can be written as the 'side relation'

$$L_{jv} = \left(\frac{b_v}{a_v}\right)^{\sigma_v} \left(\frac{r_{jv}}{w_{jv}}\right)^{\sigma_v} K_{jv} \tag{5.13}$$

where the elasticity of substitution, $\sigma_v = 1/(1 + \Phi_v)$ (see Allen, 1968, p. 53).

## Regression equations

As rewarding as the linear programming formulation has proved to be for understanding the production problem, there is little hope of obtaining sufficient empirical information to enable a solution to be derived. This section reports on an attempt to adapt the short-run macro function to a form that can be estimated using regression techniques. The most useful starting point appears to be the constraints of equation (2.3). If the production units could be observed directly, the equation might be modified to

$$Q^i = \sum_j \sum_v \xi^i_{jv} \tilde{Y}_{jv} U_{jv} = \sum_j \sum_v \psi^i_{jv} \tilde{K}_{jv} U_{jv} \qquad (5.14)$$

where $\psi^i = \dfrac{\xi^i}{\xi K}$, $U$ is a measure of capacity utilisation, and $Q^i$ is the quantity of the $i$th input used in the industry. Constant returns to the utilisation of existing capacity is assumed, otherwise $\xi = \xi(U)$ and the equation is severely complicated. This assumption also enables the analysis to switch directly between capacity, capital and labour utilisation given knowledge of $U$.

*Clay* ex ante *regime*

The case of a clay–clay technology is most straightforward. It is assumed that at any given time the various plants in the industry have only a single choice of new technology, which is given exogenously. Such a technology must improve on technologies currently embodied in the stock of inputs held by the plants or it would not be adopted. In this case,

$$\psi_{1v} = \psi_{2v} = \ldots = \psi_{mv} = \psi_v \qquad (5.15)$$

and equation (5.14) can now be written

$$L = \sum_v \psi_v K_v \qquad (5.16)$$

Here $K$ denotes the input of capital services, which are defined as

$$K_v = \tilde{K}_v U_v = \sum_j \tilde{K}_{jv} U_{jv} \qquad (5.17)$$

and $L$ denotes the input of labour services, which are defined as

$$L = \sum_v L_v = \sum_v \tilde{L}_v U_v = \sum_j \sum_v \tilde{L}_{jv} U_{jv} \qquad (5.18)$$

*Putty* ex ante *regime*

The more general case is where the *ex ante* function is characterised by the possibility of substitution between inputs. To obtain the equivalent employment function it is necessary to specify the form of the *ex ante* function. The Cobb–Douglas function and the more general CES form are separately distinguished below.

*The Cobb–Douglas function.* Using the 'side relation' [4] denoted by equation (5.11) above, knowledge of $w$ and $r$ [5] enables a weighted capital variable, $K'$, to be constructed.

$$K'_{jv} = \frac{r_{jv}}{w_{jv}} K_{jv} \qquad (5.19)$$

71

Hence, the employment relationship for the industry can be written,

$$L = \sum_j \sum_v \psi_v K'_{jv} = \sum_v \psi_v K'_v \qquad (5.20)$$

where, in this case, $\psi_v = \beta_v / \alpha_v$.

*The general CES function.* Using the 'side relation' from the more general CES function, shown as equation (5.13) above, a weighted capital variable,

$$K'_{jv} = \left(\frac{r_{jv}}{w_{jv}}\right)^{\sigma_v} K_{jv} \qquad (5.21)$$

can be constructed only where the elasticity of substitution, $\sigma_v$, is known. Given $\sigma_v$, the employment relationship can be written

$$L = \sum_j \sum_v \psi_v K'_{jv} = \sum_v \psi_v K'_v \qquad (5.22)$$

where, in this case, $\psi_v = (b_v / a_v)^{\sigma_v}$.

*Aggregation to MLHs*

Equations (5.16), (5.20) and (5.22) form the basis for functions that can be estimated cross-sectionally. The constant $\psi$ is given different interpretations according to the nature of the underlying *ex ante* regime, but in all cases the assumptions made were sufficient to allow summation across firms to take place and thereby to collapse $\psi_{jv}$ to $\psi_v$. However, in so far as the relationship holds across a number of fairly detailed industry groups (for example, MLHs), we may aggregate over firms in each industry and obtain

$$L_j = \sum_v \psi_v K_{jv} \qquad (5.23)$$

where $j$ now refers to the $j$th MLH. $K$ can simply be the total number of machines that complement the skill in question, or the number weighted by the factor-price ratio.

*The impact of disembodied technical change*

The impact of simple disembodied technical change is to modify the coefficients $\xi^K$ and $\xi^L$ at the rates $\mu$ and $\eta$ per cent per period. An additional term, $Ae^{(\mu-\eta)t}$, appears in the labour-requirements equation and at any given time appears as a scalar $B$. The labour-requirements function is now jointly multiplicative and additive of the form

$$L_j = \sum_v (B\psi_v) K_{jv} = \sum_v \psi'_v K_{jv} \qquad (5.24)$$

Linear regression techniques allow $\psi_v$ to be estimated to within a scalar while their relative values are not distorted. Alternatively, different values for $B$ can be tried, thereby estimating

$$L_j = \sum_v \psi_v (BK_{jv}) \qquad (5.25)$$

In the more complicated case where

$$L_j = \sum_v \psi_v(B_v K_{jv}) \tag{5.26}$$

the separation of $\psi_v$ and $B_v$ is even more difficult, but it would permit a check to be made whether $B_1 > \ldots > B_\tau$, $B_1 = \ldots = B_\tau$ or $B_1 < \ldots < B_\tau$.

*The role of capital usage*

A further problem concerns capital usage. Available stock figures relate to $K$ and not $KU$. Under the assumption of constant returns to usage, [6] we can write

$$K_{jv} = \tilde{K}_{jv} U_{jv} \tag{5.27}$$

and

$$L_j = \sum_v \psi_v' \tilde{K}_{jv} U_{jv} \tag{5.28}$$

The role played by usage (and the assumptions we make about the way in which capital is laid up and the returns to usage) is crucial if meaningful estimates are to be obtained. If constant returns to scale do not characterise the micro production processes, then, for example $\psi_{jv} = \psi(\tilde{Y}_{jv} - Y_{jv})$ and $\psi$ is no longer a constant.

Vintage theory suggests that $U_{jv} = 1$ when the quasi-rent arising from that production unit is non-negative, but that $U_{jv} = 0$ when it is negative. The case where inefficient behaviour occurs (i.e. where certain less efficient production units continue in operation) severely complicates matters. There is little or no data about $U_{jv}$ and this may prove of immense importance in trying to derive meaningful estimates. Indeed, even the data about industries $\left( U_j = \sum_v U_{jv} \right)$ is greatly inadequate.

## Welding: a pilot study with some lessons

The labour requirements of an individual process have been investigated in an earlier paper by the present author (see Bosworth, 1974b, pp. 177–88). Welding and metal fabrication was chosen as the subject for this pilot study, because it appeared to be a well-defined industrial activity the technology of which would not differ greatly across industries within engineering. In addition, it was a statistically well-documented process for which it was felt that labour skills and capital types could be matched with reasonable accuracy. The functions estimated in the pilot study were simplistic, but the results indicated that this approach could provide an interesting and potentially rewarding link with the Bell (1972) and Senker and Huggett (1973) studies.

The functions were based on a simple clay–clay model (although they were also consistent with a putty–clay world where all industries experience similar histories of wages and rentals). On the assumption that there was no difference between vintages, the function collapsed to the form

$$L = \rho_0 + \rho_1 K + u \tag{5.29}$$

and estimation was undertaken across industries.

An attempt was made to take account of the shiftworking problem. It was argued that at a given time an employee will work a single shift, but a unit of capital may be operated on more than one shift. The simplest approach was to adjust the total labour force, $L$, to labour employed on the main shift, $L'$, and to match this variable against the stock of equipment. This is appropriate so long as all capital is operated on the main shift. The new variable was constructed in the following way:

$$L' = L\left(1 - \frac{1}{2}\frac{L^2}{L} - \frac{2}{3}\frac{L^3}{L}\right) \tag{5.30}$$

where $L^2$ and $L^3$ denote labour employed on two- and three-shift systems, respectively. The adjustment involves subtracting one-half of labour employed on two-shift and two-thirds of labour employed on three-shift systems.

Table 5.3

Cross-sectional welding results: a simple Leontief model[a]

| Regression | Functional form | $\rho_0$ | $\rho_1$ | $\bar{R}^2$ | $F$ |
|---|---|---|---|---|---|
| (1) | $L = \psi + \rho K$ | 349·53 | 1·1430** | 0·83 | 93·96** |
| (2) | $L = \rho K$ | – | 1·0723** | – | – |
| (3) | $L' = \psi + \rho K$ | 248·78 | 1·0702** | 0·84 | 99·17** |
| (4) | $L' = \rho K$ | – | 1·0911** | – | – |

[a] The key to Table 5.1 describes the significance levels adopted.

The results of estimating these two functions for 1966 are reported in Table 5.3. The results indicated that, as extra machines are installed, the number of welders required to man them increases by a slightly greater amount. None of the $\rho_1$ coefficients is very different from unity and the difference from one-to-one manning is slightly less where shiftworking has been taken into account. Both of the functions that include constant terms have positive intercept values, but, on the basis of estimated $t$ values, in neither case are these significantly different from zero. The adjustment for shiftworking increased the overall fit of the regression very slightly (on the basis of $\bar{R}^2$ and $F$), but did not greatly affect the size or significance of the estimated coefficients. The effect of this adjustment was similar in the case of the more complex functional forms, which are not reported here.

It became apparent when using the shiftworking data that the adjustment was only very crude. First, the shift systems were not as straightforward as the calculations imply. The adjustment assumed continuous two- or three-shift systems, but in practice other types of shiftworking also existed (for instance, a four-crew three-shift system). Second, it was assumed that all equipment (which forms the stock of capital) is operated on the main (normal) shift. Third, the shiftworking data from the *Ministry of Labour Gazette* referred to manual employees and did not distinguish the nature and prevalence of systems worked by particular occupations. Finally, the survey of shiftworking related to two spot dates, 1954 and 1964, and it was the 1964 information that was used to adjust the 1966 data. This gap of two years may have led to some inaccuracies. It was not possible to interpolate and extrapolate on the basis of the 1954 and 1964 information, because of the intervening (1958) changes in industrial classification.

More complicated functional forms were tested using the 1966 data. In particular, the average age of welding machines, $V$, was included as an explanatory variable:

$$L = \rho_0 + \rho_1 K + \rho_2 V + u \tag{5.31}$$

where $V$ was constructed as a weighted average (formed by weighting by the numbers of machines in each interval the mid-points of the age intervals distinguished in the census data). Bacon and Eltis (1974), using the same information, have since shown a more appropriate method of constructing $V$. A less *ad hoc* and, from the point of view of economic theory, more easily justified function was estimated, directly distinguishing stocks of capital of various ages:

$$L = \rho + \rho_0 K_0 + \rho_1 K_1 + \rho_2 K_2 + u \tag{5.32}$$

The results of estimating both these functional forms were, however, disappointing. The *ad hoc* addition of the average age variable reduced the overall fit of the regressions (based on $\bar{R}^2$ and $F$ values) and the age variable was not significant. The addition of this variable did not, however, greatly affect the size or significance of the coefficient on capital. The subdivision of the aggregate-capital variable to distinguish a number of vintages was slightly more successful. The overall fit of the function, measured by $\bar{R}^2$, rose from approximately 0·83 to 0·94, but the estimated coefficients on capital were not meaningful. The inability to obtain significant and meaningful coefficients was partly the result of extreme multicollinearity between stocks of capital of various vintages. In retrospect, we might have expected this in a process as fundamental as welding. Industries that employed a large amount of welding equipment in the past will tend to do so in the present, unless anything unusual has happened to the timing of investment or a rapid switch away from welding has occurred in the technology of production. The effect of multicollinearity is to make the estimated coefficients individually unreliable and this makes it impossible to say anything about the nature of embodied technical change. In addition, the problem is singularly difficult to shake off.

The final regressions reported in the welding study distinguished different types of welding machines rather than different vintages of equipment. The approach appeared to be a way of taking technical change into account where it manifested itself in machines of new types (rather than different vintages of existing types). It was felt *a priori* that multicollinearity might prove less of a problem, but this was not the case. Although the reliability of the estimated coefficients was no greater, the overall fit of the regression was higher than for any of the other forms previously tested.

### Turning results

Table 5.4 reports the results of estimating equation (5.29) for turning, on the basis of the 1966, 1971 and 1966/71 pooled data. Regressions (1) show the employment of turners as a function of the stocks of lathes in engineering. The slope coefficient is considerably larger in 1971 than in 1966, but both are significant at the 1 per cent level. The overall fit of the function is better in 1971 than in 1966, but the $F$ statistics are significant at the 1 per cent level in both cases.

The results for this simple function are not as good as in the welding study. One explanation is that the match of labour skill with capital type is less appropriate. Two modifications to the function are tried. First, 'other skilled operatives' are added to 'turners', but while 'turners' tends to understate the number of workers manning lathes, the combined categories form an overestimate (because some proportion of 'other skilled operatives' man machines other than lathes). The results of modifying the dependent variable in this way are reported as regressions (2) in Table 5.4. The adjustment raises the value of the slope coefficient and the overall fit of the function is improved in both periods. Second, an attempt is made to specify more closely the type of machine that a turner might man. Turners have traditionally worked on centre lathes, and the results of modifying the independent variable in this way are reported as regressions (3) in Table 5.4. The slope coefficient is higher still. While the overall fit of the function is higher than the alternative formulations in 1966, in 1971 it is inferior to equation (2).

One further modification is to adjust the capital variable to account for the

Table 5.4

Cross-sectional turning results: a simple Leontief model[a]

| Regression | | $\rho_0$ | $\rho_1$ | $\bar{R}^2$ | $F$ |
|---|---|---|---|---|---|
| 1966 | (1) | 906·740 | 0·1896** | 0·447 | 15·54** |
| | (2) | 1832·550 | 0·4399** | 0·522 | 19·60** |
| | (3) | 259·180 | 0·7181** | 0·545 | 22·57** |
| 1971 | (1) | −314·906 | 0·4160** | 0·741 | 75·49** |
| | (2) | −239·208 | 0·9627** | 0·789 | 98·37** |
| | (3) | −427·153 | 0·9933** | 0·726 | 70·05** |
| 1966/71 | (1) | 571·019 | 0·2313** | 0·532 | 52·13** |
| | (2) | 1623·860† | 0·5228** | 0·573 | 60·13** |
| | (3) | −47·099 | 0·8103** | 0·640 | 80·88** |

[a] See key to Table 5.1.

degree of utilisation. The adjustment of $K$ by an electricity usage term, $U$, does not greatly affect the results. The slope coefficients increase slightly and the overall fit improves marginally, but the changes are not fundamental enough to justify duplicating the results.

The other variables introduced into the function in an *ad hoc* manner did not have a marked effect on the results. Table 5.5 reports estimates of the following function,

$$L = \rho_0 + \rho_1 K + \rho_2 S + \rho_3 V + \rho_4 D_0 + u \qquad (5.33)$$

where $K$ and $L$ take the alternative forms suggested above. $S$ is the percentage of employees working shifts, $V$ is the average age of capital, and $D_0$ an industry dummy. $D_0$ was included because there was a tendency for the residuals to differ between MLHs 331–49 ($D_0 = 1$) and 351–99 ($D_0 = 0$).

Table 5.5

Cross-sectional turning results: some additional variables[a]

| Regression | | $\rho_0$ | $\rho_1$ | $\rho_2$ | $\rho_3$ | $\rho_4$ | $\bar{R}^2$ | $F$ |
|---|---|---|---|---|---|---|---|---|
| 1966 | (1) | −5490·15 | 0·2641** | −172·371* | 478·901 | 2144·00† | 0·661 | 9·79** |
| | (2) | 3070·63 | 0·5402** | −248·798† | −172·202 | 6052·70* | 0·698 | 10·83** |
| | (3) | 2965·46 | 0·8047** | −32·491 | 188·062 | 1624·87 | 0·652 | 8·48** |
| 1971 | (1) | −768·97 | 0·4025** | 9·9471 | −28·9872 | 1689·69** | 0·805 | 27·82** |
| | (2) | −2198·39 | 0·9406** | 23·1182 | 17·1522 | 3224·64** | 0·831 | 32·93** |
| | (3) | −2914·92 | 1·0092** | 64·2558* | 15·1708 | 1823·57** | 0·824 | 31·45** |
| 1966/71 | (1) | 468·64 | 0·2317** | −31·5911 | −13·0247 | 2018·39** | 0·620 | 19·35** |
| | (2) | 3077·07 | 0·5205** | −26·7095 | −216·630 | 4543·28** | 0·657 | 22·03** |
| | (3) | −2033·52 | 0·8617** | 16·6544 | 59·7586 | 1789·08** | 0·758 | 34·69** |

[a] See key to Table 5.1.

The results show that the coefficient on the number of machines, $\rho_1$, is again significant at the 1 per cent level. $D_0$ is fairly consistently different from the overall constant and indicates the need, in the future, to study industry subsamples. For 1971, shiftworking has the expected positive sign (because the more shifts a given piece of capital works, the more men will be needed to man it) and is significant in regression (3), but it has a negative sign in 1966. The lack of data about various types of shiftworking and the inability to account for shiftworking carried out by various skills are particularly worrying deficiencies of $S$. The insignificant contribution made by $V$ is not too surprising given the problems associated with its measurement and the *ad hoc* nature of equation (5.33). Alternatively, $\rho_3 = 0$ can be interpreted as Hicks neutral embodied technical change ($\mu = \eta$) in a clay–clay world. The overall fit of the model (shown by $\bar{R}^2$ and $F$) has improved considerably in both periods with the addition of these variables.

Two further modifications to the function are not reported in detail. The adjustment of the capital variable by $U$ to account for variations in capital usage had

Table 5.6

Cross-sectional turning results: distinguishing vintages[a]

| Regression | | $\rho_0$ | $\rho_1$ | $\rho_2$ | $\rho_3$ | $\rho_4$ | $\rho_5$ | $\bar{R}^2$ | $F$ |
|---|---|---|---|---|---|---|---|---|---|
| 1966 | (1) | 987·261 | −0·1940 | 0·3605 | 0·8002 | −157·159* | 214·580† | 0·620 | 6·88** |
| | (2) | 750·276 | 0·3202 | 0·9044 | 0·4056 | −263·742† | 6071·43* | 0·674 | 8·04** |
| | (3) | −497·863 | −1·6181 | 1·670 | 2·3766* | −11·8406 | 1855·41 | 0·635 | 7·27** |
| 1971 | (1) | −1418·11† | 0·0808 | 1·4239** | −0·2710 | 16·5295 | 1501·23** | 0·853 | 31·11** |
| | (2) | −2674·25 | −0·7728 | 3·1646** | 0·5884 | 37·2664 | 3182·10** | 0·860 | 33·07** |
| | (3) | −1865·35 | 1·9377** | −0·8434 | 2·1749* | 39·7632 | 1546·90** | 0·847 | 29·82** |

[a] See key to Table 5.1.

78

little effect on the results, and where $U$ was included as an additional explanatory variable it was not statistically significant.

The generalisation of equation (5.3), where particular vintages are distinguished, appears as

$$L = \rho_0 + \rho_1 K_0 + \rho_2 K_1 + \rho_3 K_2 + \rho_4 S + \rho_5 D_0 + u \qquad (5.34)$$

where $K_0$ relates to capital of age 0–10 years, $K_1$ to capital of age 10–20 years, and $K_2$ to capital of age 20 or more years. The results of estimating this function for the three alternative pairings of $K$ and $L$ are reported in Table 5.6. The pooled data are no longer relevant, because the vintages 0, 1 and 2 are not the same for both 1966 and 1971.

The new results gave a slightly lower overall explanatory power for 1966 and a slightly higher one for 1971 than did the model reported in Table 5.5. The coefficients $\rho_1$, $\rho_2$ and $\rho_3$ are unstable, only occasionally significant, and impossible to interpret in a meaningful way. The reason is not hard to find. Table 5.7 shows that $K_0$, $K_1$ and $K_2$ are highly multicollinear. The extreme multicollinearity does not affect the combined contributions of $K_v$ to the overall explanation of $L$. Equations

Table 5.7

Zero-order correlation coefficients for $K_0$, $K_1$ and $K_2$, 1971

|  | All lathes | | Centre lathes | |
|---|---|---|---|---|
|  | $K_1$ | $K_2$ | $K_1$ | $K_2$ |
| $K_0$ | 0·970 | 0·888 | 0·942 | 0·856 |
| $K_1$ |  | 0·885 |  | 0·890 |

(5.33) and (5.34) are broadly similar (although equation (5.33) is an *ad hoc* formulation), and so too are their overall explanatory powers. Both models explain variations in $L$ better than equation (5.29) does.

Regressions I(1)–(3) in Table 5.8 report the results of estimating

$$L = \rho_0 + \rho_1 \left(\frac{r}{w}\right)_0^\sigma K_0 + \rho_2 \left(\frac{r}{w}\right)_1^\sigma K_1 + \rho_3 \left(\frac{r}{w}\right)_2^\sigma K_2 + \rho_4 S + \rho_5 D_0 + u \qquad (5.35)$$

where $\sigma = 1$, which is the case of the Cobb–Douglas *ex ante* function. The results, which relate to 1971, are very similar to those reported in Table 5.6. If anything, they are slightly worse in terms of overall fit: whereas regression (1) is almost identical, regressions (2) and (3) are slightly inferior. Regression II(1)–(3) in Table 5.8 report

$$L = \rho_0 + \rho_1 \left(\frac{r}{w}\right)_0^\sigma K_0 + \rho_2 \left(\frac{r}{w}\right)_1^\sigma K_1 + \rho_3 \left(\frac{r}{w}\right)_2^\sigma (K_2 U) + \rho_4 S + \rho_5 D_0 + u \qquad (5.36)$$

for $\sigma = 1$, where the only capital laid up is from the oldest vintage. The variable $(K_2 U)$ is calculated as $K_2 - (K - KU)$. Adjustment for the degree of utilisation does

Table 5.8

Cross-sectional turning results: Cobb–Douglas *ex ante* functions[a]

| Regression | | $\rho_0$ | $\rho_1$ | $\rho_2$ | $\rho_3$ | $\rho_4$ | $\rho_5$ | $\bar{R}^2$ | $F$ |
|---|---|---|---|---|---|---|---|---|---|
| I | (1) | −1039·85 | 0·6417 | 9·5384* | 1·7241 | 4·0341 | 1460·14** | 0·855 | 31·59** |
| | (2) | −211·06 | −10·4802 | 23·5907* | 15·3789* | 15·0954 | 3207·81** | 0·852 | 30·97** |
| | (3) | −1742·73 | 38·7419 | 3·3689 | 6·6921† | 50·4571 | 1614·09* | 0·721 | 14·46** |
| II | (1) | −946·71 | 1·4466 | 9·7810* | 0·5171 | 2·6032 | 1400·59** | 0·853 | 31·09** |
| | (2) | −1425·65 | −7·9962 | 25·7778** | 12·5797† | 0·6864 | 2921·89** | 0·840 | 28·32** |
| | (3) | −1632·07 | 39·2272 | 2·0856 | 10·5856* | 47·3425 | 1571·84* | 0·726 | 14·77** |

[a] See key to Table 5.1.

80

not spread to other vintages, becasue $K_2 > (K - KU)$ in every case. This adjustment corresponds to the traditional vintage model (in a world of monotonically changing factor prices) where the oldest capital is the least efficient (and the least economically viable) and hence the first to be laid up. The adjustment makes almost no difference to the results.

Given multicollinearity between $K_v$, the consistent insignificant contribution of $S$ and the generally significant contribution of $D_0$, the only basis of comparison between regressions where $\sigma$ changes is $\bar{R}^2$ and $F$. Table 5.9 shows the path of $\bar{R}^2$ as $\sigma$ changes from 0·0 to 1·2 in steps of 0·1. The first striking feature is that the $\bar{R}^2$ are all of roughly the same size. If it were necessary to choose between them, however, the Cobb–Douglas *ex ante* function would not be selected.

Table 5.9

$\bar{R}^2$ coefficients for different $\sigma$

| $\sigma$ | $\bar{R}^2$ | | |
|---|---|---|---|
| | Regression (1) | Regression (2) | Regression (3) |
| 0·0 | 0·853 | 0·861 | 0·847 |
| 0·1 | 0·858 | 0·865 | 0·874 |
| 0·2 | 0·863 | 0·868 | 0·903 |
| 0·3 | 0·866 | 0·870 | 0·915 |
| 0·4 | 0·868 | 0·871 | 0·897 |
| 0·5 | 0·868 | 0·871 | 0·863 |
| 0·6 | 0·868 | 0·870 | 0·827 |
| 0·7 | 0·866 | 0·867 | 0·780 |
| 0·8 | 0·863 | 0·863 | 0·768 |
| 0·9 | 0·859 | 0·858 | 0·743 |
| 1·0 | 0·855 | 0·852 | 0·721 |
| 1·1 | 0·848 | 0·845 | 0·701 |
| 1·2 | 0·842 | 0·836 | 0·681 |

The underlying *ex ante* function appears to have an elasticity of substitution in the region of 0·3 to 0·6. Although the results are extremely tentative, they indicate that the elasticity of substitution is, if anything, slightly lower when a more tightly defined machine type (i.e. centre lathes) is considered. The difference in $\bar{R}^2$ as $\sigma$ varies is also more distinct in the case of centre lathes, ranging from 0·681 (when a CES function with $\sigma = 1·2$ is assumed) to 0·915 (when $\sigma = 0·3$).

## Conclusions

A function based on putty–clay theory is found to provide a reasonable explanation of the numbers of turners employed by engineering industries. An important conclusion is that the *ex ante* functions, from which new technologies are chosen, have an elasticity less than unity. Elasticities in the range 0·3 to 0·6 were suggested by the results. Mayor (1969) and Johansen (1972) have pointed to the fact that time-series analyses have tended to produce elasticity estimates clustering around 0·5, whereas cross-sectional studies have produced estimates close to unity. The results contained here bear on the question of 'which of these estimates, if any, approximate the actual elasticities', although they relate to the *ex ante* function and not to an 'average' production relationship. A more tentative conclusion is that, where a number of different types of lathes are included – i.e. regressions (1) and (2) – the elasticity is slightly higher than where a specific lathe category is considered. *Ex ante* substitution appears to arise more through the choice between different types of machines than through adaptations of machines drawn from a particular category.

An important deficiency of the results is that, because of extreme multicollinearity between $K_0$, $K_1$ and $K_2$, it is not possible to isolate the role played by any particular vintage (summarised by $\hat{\psi}_0$, $\hat{\psi}_1$ and $\hat{\psi}_2$). In order to learn more about the nature and rate of embodied technological change, the problem of multicollinearity must be broken in future research. Another task for which further theoretical and empirical research is required is that of isolating and testing the significance of disembodied technical changes.

Work at micro level may prove to be particularly rewarding for economists intent on gaining insights into the nature of the technology of production. The principal barrier is the almost complete lack of detailed and accurate information, which is essential to a study of this kind.

## Notes

[1] Other dimensions, such as country of origin, are available, but are not directly relevant to this study.

[2] The average price and weight information was constructed from data given in the *Annual Statement of the Overseas Trade of the UK* and the patenting variable was taken from the *Annual Report of the Comptroller General* and *Abridgements of Specifications*.

[3] The Nadiri and Rosen study (1968) makes use of cost-minimising behaviour to yield a similar functional form, although at a more aggregate level.

[4] See Brown (1966, p. 129), Arrow et al. (1961) and Griliches and Ringstad (1971).

[5] In the past vintage theory has often assumed that there is no discrimination in wage payments to workers on different vintages of capital, $w_{j0}^i = \ldots = w_{j\tau}^i = w_j^i$. But the recent disputes about wage payments for manning jumbo jets, Concorde and advanced passenger trains are calling this assumption into question.

[6] $Y_{jv} = \dfrac{1}{\xi K_{jv}}(U_{jv}\tilde{K}_{jv}) = \dfrac{1}{\xi L_{jv}}(U_{jv}\tilde{L}_{jv}).$

# 6 Aggregate putty–clay functions

## Introduction

The empirical tests of the vintage models at a micro level are severely hampered by data constraints. At a more aggregate level, where particular industrial processes cannot be so easily distinguished, more comprehensive data are available. This information is still not ideal and there remain a number of important problems to resolve. The putty–clay function developed in Chapter 5 is now modified in order to make it as appropriate as possible, given the labour and investment data to hand. Particular labour skills and capital types are still distinguished, but the analysis is much more aggregate, being limited by the nature of the investment data available.

## Other authors' work

There is no great tradition of using investment data in empirical research on production or employment functions. Even authors who are fervent believers in the vintage approach – for instance, Johansen (1961) and Pyatt (1963) – have tended to search for ways of formulating their models in terms of more traditional (neo-classical) functional forms. Very few authors appear to have used investment data as an explanatory variable. An important reason for this lack of interest is that investment data, in the form in which they are usually published, are deficient for use in testing theoretically rigorous vintage models. Information is available about both the intensive and extensive margins, but the definitions used result in data that are far from ideal in a vintage context. In addition, in a world that fails to comply with the simple vintage models based on efficient management behaviour, the extremely detailed information required about the degree to which the various vintages are used is not available.

Only occasionally, when specific pieces of information become available, are the problems lessened. Fair (1971), for example, was able to obtain information about capacity output levels in the US cement and steel industries and to match this with the capacity labour data he was able to construct. In this way, he was able to avoid the problem of separating the short-run determinants of capacity utilisation from the long-run determinants of capital–labour substitution and the demand for capacity. 'Capacity' data, when available, allow intermediate vintages to be ignored. On the assumption that only the latest vintage can be purchased at time $t$, the Fair study formulated an employment function in first-difference terms:

D

$$\Delta \tilde{L}_t = \Phi(\Delta \tilde{Y}_t, IS_t) \tag{6.1}$$

where $\Delta$ denotes first differences, $\sim$ signifies full-capacity values and $IS$ denotes the volume of scrapping. A slight revision of the function allows net investment ($IN$) to appear in place of $\Delta Y$, but Fair found equation (6.1) better suited to the available data. In practice, an alternative formulation of the model was estimated.

$$\Delta \tilde{L}_t = \Phi\left(\Delta \tilde{Y}_t, \frac{w}{r}\right) \tag{6.2}$$

was adopted in order to test for substitution between capital and labour. This function is not quite so rigorously linked with an underlying vintage model.

Heathfield (1972b) developed a vintage model that was tested using time-series information about six UK manufacturing industries, one of which was the engineering sector. Given the assumptions of the model, theoretical rigour prevails until

$$\left(\frac{K}{L}\right)_t = \rho_0 + \rho_1 \sum_{v=1948}^{t} \frac{IG_v}{K_t} - \rho_2 \sum_{v=1948}^{t} \frac{IS_v}{K_t} + u_t \tag{6.3}$$

is obtained, but

$$\left(\frac{K}{L}\right)_t = \rho_0 + \rho_1 \sum_{v=1948}^{t} \frac{IG_v}{K_t} + \rho_2 t + \rho_3 U_t + u_t \tag{6.4}$$

is actually estimated. Here $IG$ and $IS$ denote, respectively, gross investment and scrapping; $U$ is an electricity-based measure of capital usage; $t$ is a time trend; and $u$ is the error return. Stringent assumptions underlie both models, but the functions actually estimated are only loosely connected with a vintage theory.

The final model reviewed here was presented by Lindley (1975) in an attempt to investigate the demand determinants of apprentice recruitment in the UK engineering industry. The intention was to gain an insight about whether apprentice recruitment was determined by the current production situation or whether the number of recruits was influenced by an investment motive. In much the same way as in the Heathfield (1972b) model, the relationship between capital and labour is assumed to be of a fixed-coefficient kind, [1] but substitution between apprentices and craftsmen (of the traditional log-linear form) is possible. The explanation of apprentice recruitment is formulated initially (ibid., p. 5) as a log-linear function in terms of output, relative factor prices, utilisation, and lagged apprentice recruitment. An alternative but equivalent formulation that uses capital in place of output (ibid., p. 16) is found to be equally useful:

$$L_{1t} = \Phi\left(K_t, \frac{w_{1t}}{w_{2t}}, U_t, L_{1t-1}\right) \tag{6.5}$$

where subscripts 1 and 2 refer to apprentices and craftsmen respectively. Towards the end of his paper, however, Lindley (1975, p. 19) adopted an *ad hoc* function,

$$L_{1t} = \Phi\left(IG_t, \frac{w_{1t}}{w_{2t}}, U_t, L_{1t-1}\right) \tag{6.6}$$

on the basis that, 'compared to current output ($Y_t$), gross fixed capital formation deflated by the price of capital goods ($IG_t$) would better reflect the composite pressure of current production and planned production over, say, the next three years, upon the decision to recruit apprentices ($L_{1t}$)'. The coefficient on $IG$ is significant at the 1 per cent level, and the explanatory power of this function is greater than that of its more rigorous predecessors. In so far as $L_1$ and $IG$ represent activity at the intensive margin, the results can be interpreted as giving some support to the type of vintage approach undertaken in this chapter.

## A vintage formulation

The work undertaken in Chapter 5 suggested that a function such as

$$L = \Sigma_v \psi_v \tilde{K}_v U_v \qquad (6.7)$$

could form the basis of a regression equation. The lack of data about the stock of capital in UK engineering industries suggests that it may be more useful to reformulate the equation in first-difference terms and make use of the more detailed investment data that are available. It is assumed that the set of vintages $\{0, \ldots, \tau-1\}$ are available at time $t+1$ and $\{1, \ldots, \tau\}$ at time $t$. If a new vintage is introduced in each succeeding period, equation (6.7) can be written

$$\Delta L_{t+1} = \psi_0 \tilde{K}_{0,t+1} U_{0,t+1} + \psi_1 \tilde{K}_{1,t+1} \Delta U_{1,t+1} + \ldots + \psi_{\tau-1} \tilde{K}_{\tau-1,t+1} \Delta U_{\tau-1,t+1}$$
$$- \psi_\tau \tilde{K}_{\tau,t} U_{\tau,t} \qquad (6.8)$$

where $\Delta$ denotes first differences, calculated between $t$ and $t+1$.

A number of important assumptions have been made, but a fairly realistic-looking equation has evolved. This equation suggests that the change in labour requirements between periods $t$ and $t+1$, is essentially a reflection of

(a)  the intensive and extensive coefficient ratios;
(b)  investment behaviour at the intensive and extensive margins;
(c)  the degree of capital usage at the two margins in the appropriate periods: $U_{t+1}$ and $U_t$;
(d)  the change in the degree to which intermediate vintages were utilised between $t$ and $t+1$.

The crucial role played by capital usage in the putty–clay model is now clear. However, without detailed data about individual vintages over time, there is little chance of estimating the functions given in equations (6.7) and (6.8) as they stand. In fact, we must at least make some assumptions about the manner in which capital is utilised.

## Capital usage

In Johansen's model, (1972, pp. 13–19) the short-run macro function is described as a linear programming problem, the dual of which yields the quasi-rents of the production units. Johansen's model, in common with most putty–clay models, takes the zero quasi-rent as forming the boundary between the utilised and non-utilised production units: those units with positive quasi-rents are utilised and those with negative quasi-rents are laid up. There are, in most industries, costs and uncertainties associated with the laying up of certain types of capital and also with their reinstatement after a lay-up, but these costs may be much more important in the case of tankers (see Johansen, 1972, chapter 9) than in that of machine tools.

As capital usage is a key factor in the short-run macro model, it is worth devoting some time to it. The approach reported here begins with the generally adopted economic concept of utilisation, from which more restrictive cases can be derived. The following notation is adopted: $v = 1, \ldots, \Upsilon_t^+$, denote the vintages at time $t$ that earn a positive quasi-rent; $v = \Upsilon_t^-, \ldots, \tau$, are the vintages which have negative quasi-rents. Hence, in general, we have

$$U_{vt} = 1 \quad \text{for all} \quad v = 1, \ldots, \Upsilon_t^+$$

and

$$U_{vt} = 0 \quad \text{for all} \quad v = \Upsilon_t^-, \ldots, \tau$$

It is worth emphasising that $\Upsilon$ may refer to a different vintage in different periods (i.e. when $\Upsilon_t^+$ and $\Upsilon_{t+1}^+$ appear as subscripts, they may denote different vintages of capital).

In practice it is important to assume that the productive importance of vintages with a zero quasi-rent is very small. The relevance of this assumption becomes obvious when it is remembered that such vintages are of indeterminate importance – some members of the vintage may be used and others may not. The number of these units utilised in the industry is known, but the distribution of this productive effort between plants in the industry is indeterminate.

The case being considered is most easily seen when we write out in full the demand equations for two periods:

$$L_t = \psi_1 K_1 + \ldots + \psi_{\Upsilon_t^+} \tilde{K}_{\Upsilon_t^+} \tag{6.9}$$

and

$$L_{t+1} = \psi_0 \tilde{K}_0 + \ldots + \psi_{\Upsilon_{t+1}^+} \tilde{K}_{\Upsilon_{t+1}^+} \tag{6.10}$$

These equations are based on the usual vintage concept that, in slack periods, the oldest capital is most likely to be laid up. However, under conditions where the wage–rental ratio is not a monotonically increasing function, this is by no means certain. It is useful to point out that in the equation for period $t$ the unused vintages $(v = \Upsilon_t^-, \ldots, \tau)$, where positive excess capacity exists, will generally include the vintage due to be scrapped. However, not all vintages that remain unused in this period will be scrapped. So long as their discounted streams of expected future earnings exceed the similarly discounted streams of the costs of operating them, laying them up and reintroducing them, they will be laid up rather than scrapped.

Equations (6.9) and (6.10) can be written in the difference form used earlier:

$$\Delta L_{t+1} = \psi_0 \tilde{K}_0 - \psi_\tau \tilde{K}_\tau - (\psi_{Y_{t+1}^-} \tilde{K}_{Y_{t+1}^-} + \ldots + \psi_{\tau-1} \tilde{K}_{\tau-1}$$
$$-\psi_{Y_t^-} \tilde{K}_{Y_t^-} \ldots - \psi_\tau \tilde{K}_\tau) \qquad (6.11)$$

where the terms in parentheses summarise the vintages not in use in the two periods. Equation (6.11) can now be written,

$$\Delta L_{t+1} = \psi_0 \tilde{K}_0 - \psi_\tau \tilde{K}_\tau - \left( \bar{\psi}_{t+1} \sum_{v=Y_{t+1}^-}^{\tau-1} \tilde{K}_{Y_v} - \bar{\psi}_t \sum_{v=Y_t^-}^{\tau} \tilde{K}_{Y_v} \right) \qquad (6.12)$$

where $\bar{\psi}$ denotes an average input–output ratio. Defining the summation variables from equation (6.12) as unused capital capacity, $U^k$, we have:

$$\Delta L_{t+1} = \psi_0 \tilde{K}_0 - \psi_\tau \tilde{K}_\tau - (\bar{\psi}_{t+1} U_{t+1}^k - \bar{\psi}_t U_t^k) \qquad (6.13)$$

under conditions where the technical coefficients are fairly constant, $\bar{\psi}_{t+1} \approx \bar{\psi}_t$, and the final term of equation (6.13) appears as $\bar{\psi} (\Delta U_{t+1}^k)$. If the set of utilised vintages forms the whole capital stock in both periods, then the terms that appear in parentheses on the right-hand side of equation (6.13) are zero. Thus (6.13) reduces to

$$\Delta L_{t+1} = \psi_0 K_0 - \psi_\tau K_\tau \qquad (6.14)$$

which is an interesting special case.

*Short-run adjustment*

Unfortunately, if $t$ and $t+1$ refer to consecutive quarters or even years, estimates of the equilibrium values of the parameters ($\psi_v$) are likely to be distorted by the incomplete adjustment of $L$ to $K$. Although it should be possible to obtain estimates of the adjustment process and the long-run equilibrium values by adding an adjustment mechanism and pooling the time-series and cross-sectional dimensions of the data, this study attempts the simpler procedure of reducing the relative importance of the adjustment process by lengthening the gap between $t$ and $t+1$ (to, say, three, five or even seven years). The problem is that, the longer the gap between $t$ and $t+1$, the less homogeneous will any particular $K_v$ become (where $K_0 = \sum_{v=t}^{t+1} IG_v$ and $K_\tau = \sum_{v=t}^{t+1} IS_v$) and the more will $\psi_v$ appear as average input ratios rather than as technical coefficients associated with distinct vintages. It was decided to try a five-year gap between $t$ and $t+1$. As labour data were based on mid-year estimates of employment, and investment was taken over a calendar year, $\sum_{1963}^{67} I$ was matched with $\Delta L_{63, 68}$, which in effect allowed a six-month lag between investment and the date for meeting manning targets. A time series of parameter estimates was again obtained by removing the first year of a sample and adding on the next year available (i.e. $\Delta L_{63, 68}, \Delta L_{64, 69}, \ldots \Delta L_{67, 72}$ are matched with $\sum_{63}^{67} I$, $\sum_{64}^{68} I$, ..., $\sum_{67}^{71} I$, respectively).

**Data availability**

UK investment data are far from ideal for estimating even the simplest vintage function. In addition to total investment, only three types of investment goods are distinguished (plant and machinery, vehicles, and buildings). Intuition suggested that it might be appropriate to match 'all workers' with total investment, 'craftsmen' with plant and machinery, and 'drivers' with vehicles investment. The labour data (recorded in thousands of employees), are again taken from the survey carried out by the Engineering Industry Training Board in conjunction with the Department of Employment, while the investment data (recorded in £ million) are based on the annual 'sample' and quinquennial 'full' censuses.

Data about acquisitions and disposals are available for plant and machinery and for vehicles, but not for buildings (except in recent years) and therefore not for total investment. MLH data are not published except in quinquennial census years and in the annual censuses from 1970 onwards. Information from the sample censuses can be traced back to 1948 for seven engineering industries, which correspond broadly to the 1968 Standard Industrial Classification (SIC) groups. Appendix I describes how the sample and full censuses can be combined to produce MLH detail annually from 1958 by type of investment good. Although the method of construction leaves much to be desired, the resulting MLH data should adequately reflect the levels of investment undertaken.

The published investment data are in current prices. Ideally, however, the vintage model requires information about the volume of investment, and an attempt to adjust the data for changes in prices must be made. The only reliable price information that is available is the implicit deflator used in the *Blue Book*. Even this information is not adequate: where constant and current prices are both distinguished (enabling the implicit deflator to be calculated) the relevant detail treats industry subgroups and types of investment goods separately, and not in combination. This study chooses to use a different deflator for each type of investment good, but to assign to each deflator the same value for all engineering industries. There are obvious problems and sources of potential error in not distinguishing a separate index for each industry and type of investment good. This study is forced to adjust acquisitions and disposals by the same index of prices, although the index for second-hand machines may differ from that for new equipment, and this may be a further source of measurement error.

The final problem is perhaps even more crucial. Acquisitions (purchases) and disposals (sales) do not correspond to the theoretical concepts of gross investment and scrapping. Acquisitions may include purchases of machines that are not of the latest vintage, and disposals may not all be of the vintage being scrapped. [2] (This problem was touched on in Chapter 3.) However, it is probably true to say that acquisitions will tend to be associated with machines of the latest vintage, and disposals with older vintages.

Capital-usage data based on the consumption of electricity have been reported briefly in earlier chapters. An attempt is made here to match different types of fuel with different types of capital. Usage figures for 'all investment' are based on percentage deviations from linear trends (one for each MLH) estimated from data on total fuel consumption. Usage data for 'plant and machinery' and for 'vehicles' are based on the consumption of 'electricity' and of 'all liquid fuels', respectively. The construction of the fuel-consumption data used in estimating usage series is described in Appendix II. The method of constructing usage series has been described in some detail by Evans (1974).

## Results

The results obtained when estimating the simplest function,

$$\Delta L = \rho_0 + \rho_1 \sum IN + u \qquad (6.15)$$

are reported in Tables 6.1, 6.2 and 6.3 for all workers, for craftsmen and for drivers, respectively. The results are not very impressive. The coefficient on net investment is generally insignificantly different from zero and tends to be unstable over time. In addition, the overall fit of the regressions (measured by $\bar{R}^2$ and $F$) is not particularly good.

Table 6.1

All labour and total net investment[a]

| Period | $\rho_0$ | $\rho_1$ | $\bar{R}^2$ | $F$ |
|--------|----------|----------|-------------|-----|
| 1961–65 | −4·0520 | 0·1727** | 0·32 | 15·04** |
| 1962–66 | −3·2678 | 0·1086** | 0·24 | 10·67** |
| 1963–67 | −1·7296 | 0·0836* | 0·16 | 6·62** |
| 1964–68 | −2·5096 | 0·0758* | 0·13 | 5·55* |
| 1965–69 | 20·4484* | −0·4701** | 0·61 | 48·17** |
| 1966–70 | −7·7658† | 0·0488 | 0·03 | 1·84 |
| 1967–71 | −14·2254† | 0·0229 | – | 0·16 |

[a] See key to Table 5.1.

Table 6.2

Craftsmen and investment in plant and machinery[a]

| Period | $\rho_0$ | $\rho_1$ | $\bar{R}^2$ | $F$ |
|--------|----------|----------|-------------|-----|
| 1963–67 | 2·3210 | 0·0432 | 0·02 | 1·51 |
| 1964–68 | −0·3692 | 0·0127 | – | 0·30 |
| 1965–69 | −0·2940 | 0·0144 | – | 0·33 |
| 1966–70 | −3·5816 | 0·0222 | – | 0·86 |
| 1967–71 | −7·5991* | 0·0873** | 0·20 | 7·62** |

[a] See key to Table 5.1.

Table 6.3

Drivers and vehicles investment[a]

| Period | $\rho_0$ | $\rho_1$ | $\bar{R}^2$ | $F$ |
|--------|----------|----------|-------------|-----|
| 1963–67 | 0·1220 | 0·1411** | 0·32 | 15·39** |
| 1964–68 | 0·0759 | 0·0104 | – | 0·27 |
| 1965–69 | 0·0149 | 0·0472** | 0·45 | 25·56** |
| 1966–70 | 0·0413 | 0·0288 | 0·03 | 1·79 |
| 1967–71 | 0·0347 | 0·0130 | – | 0·68 |

[a] See key to Table 5.1.

The results for all labour are the most promising. The coefficient on the investment term declines over the period (with the exception of one particularly large jump, which is difficult to explain) and is significant in five out of seven cases (although one of these, 1965–69, has an unexpected sign). The $F$ statistics are significant at the 5 per cent level or better in the same five cases. The results indicate that an extra £1 million of net investment had the effect of creating an extra 173 jobs in engineering in the period 1961–65. This already fairly small impact of investment on overall employment in engineering became negligible by the end of the period.

The results for craftsmen and for drivers are even less impressive. The overall fit of the regressions are extremely poor and the slope coefficients are generally insignificant, which makes them extremely difficult to interpret. In both cases, the direct impact of £1 million net investment (i.e. on the labour skill directly associated with that capital type) is to create a small number of jobs. £1 million net investment in plant and machinery creates an extra 43 craftsmen jobs in the 1963–67 period, but 87 in 1967–71. The same additional investment in vehicles produces jobs for 141 drivers in 1963–67, but fewer towards the end of the period.

The inclusion of an extra term for changes in capital usage (based on total fuel for all investment, electricity for plant and machinery, and liquid fuels for vehicles investment), in the form

$$\Delta L_t = \rho_0 + \rho_1 \sum IN + \rho_2 \Delta U + u \qquad (6.16)$$

makes little difference to the results overall. $\Delta U$ is insignificant for every period for craftsmen and drivers, but slightly better for all labour. The results for the aggregate labour group are reported in Table 6.4, but even in this case $\Delta U$ is significant at the 10 per cent level or better in only two instances.

Tables 6.5 and 6.6 report the results relating to craftsmen and drivers for the slightly more complicated case where net investment is divided into two parts: gross investment ($\sum IG$) and replacement investment ($\sum IS$). The functional form estimated is

$$\Delta L = \rho_0 + \rho_1 \sum IG + \rho_2 \sum IS + u \qquad (6.17)$$

90

Table 6.4

All labour, accounting for changes in capital usage[a]

| Period | $\rho_0$ | $\rho_1$ | $\rho_2$ | $\bar{R}^2$ | $F$ |
|---|---|---|---|---|---|
| 1961–65 | −3·9380 | 0·1733** | −0·0562 | 0·295 | 7·29** |
| 1962–66 | −3·8352 | 0·1101** | 0·2094 | 0·226 | 5·37 |
| 1963–67 | −2·4606 | 0·0859* | 0·2740 | 0·197 | 3·43 |
| 1964–68 | −5·4055 | 0·0751* | 0·5012 | 0·184 | 4·36 |
| 1965–69 | 14·7005 | −0·4552** | 1·2975† | 0·636 | 27·23** |
| 1966–70 | −5·2783 | 0·0499 | 0·5957† | 0·107 | 2·79 |
| 1970–71 | −14·5657 | 0·0251 | −0·0553 | – | 0·10 |

[a] See key to Table 5.1.

Table 6.5

Craftsmen – acquisitions and disposals of plant and machinery[a]

| Period | $\rho_0$ | $\rho_1$ | $\rho_2$ | $\bar{R}^2$ | $F$ |
|---|---|---|---|---|---|
| 1963–67 | 0·6576 | 0·0118 | 0·9250 | 0·016 | 1·25 |
| 1964–68 | 1·6550 | 0·0613† | −1·3585† | 0·041 | 1·64 |
| 1965–69 | 2·1543 | 0·0605† | −1·4221† | 0·057 | 1·91 |
| 1966–70 | 1·4904 | 0·0978** | −2·5488** | 0·305 | 7·15** |
| 1967–71 | −0·0441 | 0·2208** | −4·1882** | 0·534 | 16·48** |

[a] See key to Table 5.1.

Table 6.6

Drivers – acquisitions and disposals of vehicles[a]

| Period | $\rho_0$ | $\rho_1$ | $\rho_2$ | $\bar{R}^2$ | $F$ |
|---|---|---|---|---|---|
| 1963–67 | −0·0607 | −0·2156 | 0·8201 | 0·357 | 9·33** |
| 1964–68 | 0·1100 | −0·1472 | 0·4120 | – | 0·94 |
| 1965–69 | 0·0186 | −0·0600 | 0·2476 | 0·501 | 16·09** |
| 1966–70 | −0·0364 | −0·1947 | 0·6632† | 0·332 | 6·96** |
| 1967–71 | 0·1484 | −0·2953** | 0·8046** | 0·264 | 6·38** |

[a] See key to Table 5.1.

where $L$ relates to craftsmen and $I$ is plant and machinery investment, or where drivers are matched with vehicles. Separating the two components of investment improves the results. Only the 1966–70 and 1967–71 craftsmen results are acceptable both in terms of their overall fit and the significance of coefficients, but in addition the 1964–68 and 1965–69 coefficients are accepted at the 10 per cent level as being significantly different from zero. The coefficients for all periods except 1963–67 have the expected sign. The drivers results, on the other hand, give significant $F$ statistics in four out of the five cases, but the slope coefficients are really acceptable only in 1967–71. The slope coefficients have unexpectedly negative signs on $IG$ and positive signs on $IS$ because of the extremely strong multicollinearity between $IG$ and $IS$ that characterises vehicles investment. Table 6.7 shows the extent of the

Table 6.7

Zero-order correlation coefficients – $r_{IS, IG}$

| Period | Investment types | |
| | Plant and machinery | Vehicles |
|---|---|---|
| 1963–67 | 0·694 | 0·995 |
| 1964–68 | 0·800 | 0·995 |
| 1965–69 | 0·738 | 0·995 |
| 1966–70 | 0·743 | 0·992 |
| 1967–71 | 0·795 | 0·996 |

multicollinearity problem by giving the zero-order correlation coefficients for the two cases. The extreme multicollinearity, particularly in the case of vehicles, is shown by zero-order correlation coefficients in excess of 0·99.

The craftsmen regressions appear to give rise to the most reliable estimates of the coefficients. With the exception of 1963–67 they indicate that a given value of investment ($IG$) creates only one job for approximately every 20 that an equal value of scrapping ($IS$) loses. In 1966–70, for example, an additional £1 million of acquisitions creates 98 jobs, while the same value of scrapping releases 2,549 employees. Multicollinearity may be playing a part in making the estimated coefficients, and hence their relative values, unreliable. Part of the explanation of the small 'creation-release' ratio is that, because older machines tend to command a lower price – particularly where transport costs of transferring second-hand machines have to be met out of future earnings – there are more machines scrapped per £1 million than can be purchased for that amount. The implication is that, even if the price index adopted here has adequately coped with translating variations in values over time to equivalent variations in volume for both new and second-hand machines, it has failed to make the magnitudes of new to second-hand machines reflect their relative volumes.

## Conclusions

This chapter has attempted to develop a labour-demand equation relevant to the UK engineering industries and capable of being estimated using the rather limited data available for UK industries. It cannot be denied that some of the assumptions that it proved necessary to make in order to isolate this function were stringent. Nevertheless, the final functional forms – shown above as equations (6.13) and (6.14) – did appear to be both intuitively plausible and empirically testable. The results reported do not provide overwhelming evidence in support of the vintage hypothesis. On the other hand, despite the existence of important theoretical and empirical problems, the results indicate that further research along these lines may well prove rewarding.

The models appear to provide a basis for making forecasts of labour requirements. Given an appropriate pool of data, the cross-sectional analysis can be repeated for a number of years. With a sufficiently long time series of estimates of the technology coefficients, explanatory variables may be found that could be used to predict future values of the coefficients. These could then be used in a simulation exercise (with alternative time paths of output, capacity utilisation and investment) to produce conditional forecasts of future manpower requirements. Such an approach would avoid Blaug's criticism of single-valued forecasts (see Blaug, 1967 and 1970).

If the approach is eventually to provide models that are accurate descriptions of past changes in employment and are useful in forecasting exercises, a number of important data problems must be resolved. First, price indices are needed that relate to different industries and types of investment and distinguish new from second-hand investment goods. Second, the data on acquisitions and disposals must be modified. It is really necessary to have separate information about purchases of second-hand equipment. Data on disposals should similarly distinguish between sales and scrapping of capital. Third, where original values and second-hand values differ they should be separately distinguished. This is particularly important in the case of capital being scrapped, because this will generally have no second-hand value. Fourth, it would be extremely helpful to know the ages of machines being traded or scrapped.

The method of constructing MLH investment data for use in this study was far from ideal. Since 1970, however, information has become available at the MLH level (and even for certain MLH subgroups). There is some evidence in Tables 6.5 and 6.6 that the results for later years are better than for earlier years, but obviously the improved investment data may not be the only contributory factor.

The MLH fuel data, on which the capital-usage series were based, also were based on inadequate data. In this case, the published information does not become more detailed in more recent years. Estimates of capital usage for different types of capital could be made much more accurate given more detail in the fuel-consumption series. One problem that must be faced squarely, however, is that usage data are unlikely ever to distinguish the intensity with which particular vintages are worked (except perhaps at a very micro level). Given the key role that capital usage plays in a vintage model, this may prove a crucial deficiency, and the inclusion of such data will generally be associated with a lack of theoretical rigour.

There are a number of other improvements that can be made, though they have not been attempted in this chapter. The problems of matching labour skills with machine types has not been discussed here in detail and in practice requires more experimentation. A related problem is to attempt to trace the secondary employment effects of various investment decisions (i.e. through skill groups not directly linked with that investment good). There are a number of other explanatory variables that have not been tested in this chapter (for instance, shiftworking), and, in addition, some simple tests of inter-industry differences (for instance, between SICs) could have been made. Finally, by pooling the time-series and cross-sectional dimensions of the data (or simply by concentrating on the time-series dimension), estimates of the short-run adjustment might have been made. This would have involved some assumption about the nature of embodied technical change (for example, exponential), but would have meant that $\hat{\psi}_0$ and $\hat{\psi}_\tau$ were not average values over a five-year period. The larger data base might have reduced the degree of multicollinearity between $IG$ and $IS$.

## Notes

[1] Both Heathfield (1972b) and Lindley (1975) adopted the aggregate production functions by analogy with micro theory. Lindley (1974, p. 6) pointed out that the conditions for rigorous aggregation across firms are invariably not met. However, Johansen's 1972 study emphasised that aggregate functions need not have the same form as the underlying micro technologies and that often the micro–macro analogy will be misleading.

[2] It is likely that the machines with positive second-hand value will not have reached the end of their economic working lives. While a machine earning a zero quasi-rent in one industry may command a positive second-hand value (for instance, in an industry with lower labour costs), this seems unlikely to be common, because the higher gross profitability of the machine in the new industry must cover the costs of transferring the machine between firms.

# 7 Aggregate neoclassical production functions

## Introduction

This chapter reports evidence about the empirical performance of neoclassical production functions, when estimated using data drawn from the UK engineering industry. [1] The functions are aggregate in the sense that they relate to all production processes carried out within an industry: particular capital types and labour skills are not distinguished. However, this cross-MLH study is concerned with a more homogeneous sample of industries than has been studied by other authors (see, for example, Feldstein, 1967). Thus, despite the rather aggregate nature of the estimates, certain features of the technology may still be apparent. Sawyer (1970), for example, has argued that the UK industrial groupings used in the compilation of official statistics are based more on the technology of production than on any considerations of market structure.

If the neoclassical formulation is accepted as realistic, then repeated cross-sectional estimation for a number of consecutive years should enable changes in output caused by a shift in the production function to be isolated from those arising from movements around a given function. Nelson (1973) has argued that it is a major criticism of growth-accounting exercises that they have been forced to assume the form of the production function in order to separate changes in output resulting from changes in factor supplies from those caused by changes in technical efficiency. Estimating production functions at different points in time gives rise to a time series of technology parameters, with the possibility of explaining their past movements and projecting them into the future. If this could be achieved successfully, it could have important implications for planning and forecasting exercises.

The main thrust of the exercise undertaken here, however, is not an attempt to work within a neoclassical world, but an attempt to provide some evidence of the limitations of neoclassical thought. The neoclassical variables are not dismissed as irrelevant, but are shown to be only part of a more complex description of the real world. The work undertaken here is only the starting point. It is severely hampered by data problems and by the lack of an adequate theoretical basis for describing the real world. While some initial steps are made in the next chapter to back up the results found here, there is little more that can be done on an empirical front until adequate data become available.

## Aggregate production functions

Neoclassical theoretical and empirical research has become particularly interested in the CES class of functions. The Cobb–Douglas function, which is a special case of the CES class, has obvious practical advantages in estimation, because its log-linear form lends itself readily to simple linear regression techniques. The general CES function, where the elasticity of substitution is not preconstrained to unity,

$$Y = \zeta [aK^{-\Phi} + bL^{-\Phi}]^{-\theta/\Phi} \qquad (7.1)$$

has combined multiplicative and additive terms that make it extremely difficult to estimate by simple regression techniques. $\zeta$ is a technical efficiency parameter, $a$ and $b$ denote factor shares, and $\theta$ is the returns-to-scale parameter.

The pioneering study by Arrow et al. (1961) estimated the 'side relation',

$$\log\left(\frac{Y}{L}\right) = c + \sigma \log w \qquad (7.2)$$

where $c$ is a constant and $\sigma$ denotes the elasticity of substitution.

Equation (7.2) can be obtained by manipulating the production function under the assumption of cost-minimising behaviour. A major advantage of estimating this functional form is that the elasticity of substitution, $\sigma$, enters as a first-order parameter and there is more chance of estimating it with some precision. Brown (1966) has argued, however, that not all of the parameters of the production function appear in the equation, and has suggested (ibid., pp. 128–33) that the remaining parameters could be estimated by adopting a two-stage procedure. This involves first estimating the 'side-relation' in terms of the equation for the expansion path,

$$\log\left(\frac{K}{L}\right) = d - \sigma \log\left(\frac{r}{w}\right) \qquad (7.3)$$

Using the results from this equation, $\sigma$ and $b/a$ can be estimated. On the assumption that $b = 1 - a$, and knowing that $\sigma = \dfrac{1}{1+\Phi}$ we have sufficient information to construct a new variable,

$$(\hat{KL}) = (aK^{-\Phi} + bL^{-\Phi}) \qquad (7.4)$$

and equation (7.1) can be rewritten as

$$\log Y = \log \zeta - \frac{\theta}{\Phi} \log(\hat{KL}) \qquad (7.5)$$

This enables $\zeta$ and $\theta$ to be estimated.

Of course, if we are willing to adopt an iterative procedure (as opposed to a two-stage procedure), it is possible to estimate functions that are more general than CES. Brown (1966, p. 135) reports some work by Hilhorst, who suggested

$$Y = \zeta [aK^{\Phi\kappa} + bL^{\Phi_L}]^{1/\Phi} \qquad (7.6)$$

as a more general formulation in the sense that it is non-homogeneous where $\Phi_K = \Phi_L$; it is homogeneous of degree $\theta/\Phi$ where $\Phi_K = \Phi_L = \theta$; and it is linearly homogeneous with $\sigma = \dfrac{1}{1+\Phi}$ where $\Phi_K = \Phi_L = \Phi$. The function is estimated by an iterative procedure centring on $\hat{\Phi}_K$ and $\hat{\Phi}_L$, which Hilhorst found to converge to constant values very rapidly.

The essential problem with the two-stage and the iterative approaches is that they rely on two theories: a theory of the firm and a theory of the technology of production. In Chapter 5 the limitations of the data made it impossible to avoid making an assumption about managerial behaviour, but no such limitations constrain the study at this level of aggregation, and other methods of estimating neoclassical functions do exist. A secondary problem is that the introduction of a theory of the firm implies the need for data about factor prices, and such data often are not available at a detailed level. The Hilhorst study had slightly fewer difficulties in this respect, because it required information only about relative factor shares.

Direct estimation of the technical relationship requires the acceptance of one theory instead of two. The function can be estimated directly by expanding equation (7.6) using Taylor's theorem. The idea was put forward by Brown (1966, pp. 133–4), but his estimates were based on an iterative procedure where each iteration involved a least-squares estimate. An advantage of this approach is that, if the iterations produce estimates that converge, the parameter estimates and their standard errors are those of the non-linear equation. Kmenta (1967), however, has produced a version where repeated estimation is avoided. Equation (7.1) is rewritten

$$\frac{Y}{L} = \zeta L^{\theta-1} \left[ a\left(\frac{K}{L}\right)^{-\Phi} + b \right]^{-\theta/\Phi} \tag{7.7}$$

and expansion around $\Phi = 0$, using Taylor's theorem, yields

$$\log\left(\frac{Y}{L}\right) = a_0 + a_1 \log L + a_2 \log\left(\frac{K}{L}\right) + a_3 \left[ \log\left(\frac{K}{L}\right) \right]^2 \tag{7.8}$$

where $a_0 = \log$; $a_1 = \theta - 1$; $a_2 = \theta b$; $a_3 = \frac{1}{2}\theta ab\Phi$. The function collapses to the equivalent Cobb–Douglas form when $a_3$ is insignificantly different from zero. Following Griliches and Ringstad (1971, pp. 7–10) this study adopts equation (7.8) as a direct test of the Cobb–Douglas function.

There are problems with the approach. Griliches and Ringstad (1971, pp. 9–10), for example, pointed to the fact that the expansion was carried out around $\Phi \neq 0$ (i.e. $\sigma = 1$) and the approximation is better the closer the elasticity of substitution is to unity. Unfortunately, the further the elasticity is from unity, the more important the higher-order terms (which have been omitted) become. In this case, $a_3 \neq 0$ may imply production functions outside the CES class. A second problem arises from the small size of $a_3$ (as it is formed as the product of at least two parameters that are less than unity). The implication is that we are likely to need large samples and an adequate dispersion of $(K/L)$ to say anything about the sign and magnitude of $a_3$. Third, the parameter estimates of $a_1$ and $a_2$ (and by implication $a$, $b$ and $\sigma$) are not independent of the units by which we measure $K$ and $L$. Griliches and Ringstad (1971, p. 10) proposed that we evaluate the elasticities at the (geometric) mean levels of the inputs and, in particular, at a level where the geometric means of the sample are equal; i.e. $\overline{K} = \overline{L}$ and $\log(\overline{K}/\overline{L}) = \log(1) = 0$.

The data base for this study is relatively large, with information available about 32 MLHs in each year. In addition, where it appears necessary, cross-sectional and time-series dimensions of the data can be pooled for some or all of the 12 years for which data are available. The data should be more than adequate to obtain a precise estimate of the coefficient $a_3$ if the higher-order terms make a significant contribution to the explanation of variations in output per head. This study follows Griliches and Ringstad (1971) and interprets the elasticities at the mean levels of the sample. As the alternative techniques for estimating neoclassical functions are much more complicated and time consuming, it was decided to resort to them only if $a_3$ were statistically significant.

If it proves necessary to re-estimate the function, there are two main alternatives. The first of these is to adopt a non-linear estimation technique; for example, the one used by Leech (1975). The main problem is that it approaches the minimum squared deviations by making use of information about the gradient of the initial curve fitted. Hill-climbing methods of this type imply that the standard statistical tests are not valid and force the researcher to use asymptotic tests (i.e. those that are true when the sample size grows very large), which are not really applicable to small sample sizes. The other alternative is to use a simple search procedure that uses alternative values of key parameters in the estimation of other parameters. From equation (7.1), for example, we might try alternative values of $\Phi$ and $\theta$ in a two-dimensional search for the minimum variance. There are two immediate problems with this approach: first, the relevance of searching for the minimum variance; second, the sheer size of the search, which raises important practical problems. [2]

**The basic formulation, explanatory variables and sources of data**

In the simplest case reported here estimates are obtained on the assumption that all of the MLHs can be treated as though consistent with the same technology of production. The general form of the function can be written

$$Y_{jt} = Y_t(K_{jt}, L_{jt}, H_{jt}) \tag{7.9}$$

where $Y$ denotes value-added, $K$ the input of capital services, $L$ the number of employees, and $H$ the hours that they work. There are both theoretical and practical problems in obtaining meaningful measures of all the variables that appear in the function.

*The output variable*

This study follows the convention of adopting a value-added measure of output. The data are constructed from annual indices of industrial production for the period after 1958. The statistics for individual MLHs are intended to reflect the volume of industrial production over time, and, hence, no adjustment need be made for changes in prices. However, before the data can be used in cross-sectional studies of production, weights that reflect the relative magnitudes of the outputs of the various industries have to be applied to the individual index-number series. The 1963 weights prepared by the Central Statistical Office, based on the net value of output, were chosen for use in this study. The general form of the function adopted does not separately distinguish the input of raw materials, and this implies that we should adopt a value-added measure of output, although this is associated with an important measurement problem (see Klein, 1962, p. 97). The output data used in this chapter are confidential and therefore are not reported in detail. Over 30 MLHs that the 1968 SIC classification defined as belonging to engineering are distinguished. The information relates to 1961–72 inclusive – a span of twelve years.

*The capital input*

Perpetual inventory estimates of the capital stock have all too often proved inadequate to the needs of the large and growing interest in the empirical investigation of production. The lack of useful data becomes increasingly apparent at greater levels of disaggregation, and yet it is at these levels that some of the more interesting aspects of production become apparent. The inadequacies of the data are not too surprising given the enormous amount of detailed and accurate information that is required for the construction of traditional measures. The post-war gross stocks of capital reported in Pyatt (1964b) and Armstrong (1974) are calculated as the cumulative amount of investment over a period equal to the life expectancy of capital.

The inadequacies of perpetual inventory information have forced researchers to use proxy variables such as time trends (see, for example, Ball and St Cyr, 1966) and fuel-consumption measures (see Bosworth, 1974b, pp. 165–77, and Moody, 1974). The fuel-consumption proxy has a certain intuitive appeal and, since its use by Foss (1963), has grown considerably in stature. In the recent economics literature, electricity consumption has been used as a proxy for the consumption of capital services. Taylor (1967) reported a high correlation between electricity consumption and active capital stock across regions in the UK. Heathfield (1972) compared the consumption of electricity with the stock of capital, where the book value of capital was taken to be a measure of the potential supply of capital services. Bosworth (1974b, pp. 189–90) allocated the SIC value of capital among MLHs in accord with their relative fuel consumptions. Finally, Moody (1974) has argued that the fuel proxy is generally a more useful and accurate measure that are its perpetual-inventory counterparts, which often are constructed in a roundabout way and generally on the basis of inadequate information. As far as this study is concerned, there is little choice other than to adopt a fuel-consumption proxy, because the available perpetual-inventory estimates relate to much higher levels of aggregation, and the time-trend proxy is inappropriate in this (cross-sectional) context.

A fuel-based proxy is unlikely to be useful in representing the stock of capital in its role as a measure of the store of wealth. On the other hand, it does appear to be a relevant proxy for the input of capital in the context of a production relationship. In particular, it allows two identical plants, worked at the same capacity, to have the same measure of the capital input even where their factor prices differ (see Solow, 1956, p. 101). The fuel-based measure of the capital input should enable detailed cross-sectional work to be undertaken for a number of years. The method used in constructing the fuel data, which have already been used in this study, is reported in Appendix II. One important point that must be emphasised is that fuel proxies reflect the consumption of capital services and not the stock of capital. Recent work on employment functions, such as that undertaken by Feldstein (1967) and Craine (1972), have separated employees' hours from numbers employed, and the question arises of whether the stock of capital and capital usage should be separately distinguished: it is, after all, particular human characteristics associated with the length of the working day that make the employment–hours split necessary. One thing is certain, however: where only a fuel proxy is available it is not possible to include both variables in the regression.

This is perhaps an opportune point to note that there does exist a strong relationship between the alternative measures of capital. Two particular tests were made: one investigating the relationship between numbers of machine tools and fuel consumption; the other investigating the relationship between cumulative investment and fuel consumption. The results of these tests are not reported in detail, but there existed strong relationships in both cases and these relationships were closer where particular types of capital were matched with particular fuel categories (i.e. all fuels with total net investment; electricity with plant and machinery; liquid fuels with vehicles). These tests were reassuring in the sense that, even where we expect fuel-based measures to be an improvement on the other capital variables in this context, we expect there to be a fairly close relationship between them.

*The labour input*

Obviously, a firm can change its level of activity, *ceteris paribus*, by increasing or decreasing the number of people it employs. Annual information about the numbers employed by MLHs, distinguishing males and females separately, has been available since 1948. Since 1963, the survey carried out by the Department of Employment in conjunction with the Engineering Industry Training Board has been the source of this information, and in addition to the existing dimensions has distinguished occupations. This chapter uses only the total labour input, constructed using information taken from the *Historical Abstract of Labour Statistics* and the *Labour Yearbook*.

It has long been recognised (see, for example, the work of Douglas, 1948) that the *ceteris paribus* condition imposed above is invalid. Variations in output can be caused by changes in the length of the working week with a given labour force. The hours variable used in this study is formed as a weighted average of male and female hours, where the weights applied are the relative sizes of male and female employment. The separate elements are aggregated additively, which may not be theoretically rigorous in multiplicative functions, and the marginal products of male and female hours are assumed equal. The information used is from the same source as the labour data.

A third dimension to the input of labour services is the intensity with which the labour force works. It is unlikely that we can obtain any simple summary measure of effort, because the influences on this aspect of the labour input are likely to be diverse and not easily quantified. We might expect effort to be related to the number of hours worked, the nature of the shift system, labour bonus schemes, and so on. There are physical, intellectual and mental limits to the performance of labour (the recent work on circadian time may, for example, tell us something about the most appropriate type of shift system) as well as organisational and workplace limits (for instance, relationships with superiors and workmates). These features are unlikely to be introduced explicitly into the production relationship except at the most micro level.

This aspect of the labour input has close connections with Liebenstein's work on 'X-efficiency' (see Liebenstein, 1966 and 1969), and Dudley et al. (1968) have shown, on the basis of evidence drawn from the engineering industries, that this pheno-menon may be empirically important. Hoarding data (see, for example, Evans, 1974, pp. 115–47) may pick up some part of this inefficiency. Hoarding reached quite large proportions within the engineering industries at various times in the 1960s and early 1970s; but, as work in this area has emphasised, the static inefficiencies that arise through hoarding may result in dynamic gains (see Evans, 1974, pp. 123–5). It may, for example, be less costly to hoard labour in a temporary downturn than to make someone redundant and obtain a new employee (who may need experience and training) at a later date. Liebenstein's theory of 'inert areas' suggests that competitive forces, firm size and other structural variables may have an important bearing on the pressures placed on management (through the degree of account-ability to shareholders, the fear of losing a managerial post, and so on) and the ability of management to motivate their workers. These factors may differ between industry groups and, to the extent that they do, may be picked up using industry dummies, subdividing the sample by industry group or by the inclusion of structural variables.

### Aggregate cross-sectional results

*Annual, cross-sectional production functions*

This section concentrates on the results obtained from estimating a number of aggregate production functions across all industries within engineering. The

101

functions are re-estimated for each year of the sample period (1961, 1962, ..., 1972). The results for the Cobb–Douglas function,

$$Y_{jt} = A_t K_{jt}^{\alpha_t} L_{jt}^{\beta_t} \tag{7.10}$$

are reported in Table 7.1. The explanatory power of the function (measured by $\bar{R}^2$

Table 7.1

Annual Cobb–Douglas functions[a]

| Year | log $A$ | $\alpha$ | $\beta$ | $(\alpha + \beta)$ | $\bar{R}^2$ | $F$ | $(\bar{R}^2)$ |
|------|---------|----------|---------|-------------------|-------------|-----|---------------|
| 1961 | 1·8588** | 0·2557* | 0·7977** | (1·0534) | 0·91 | 155·16** | (0·078) |
| 1962 | 1·8064** | 0·2207* | 0·8408** | (1·0615) | 0·92 | 167·87** | (0·072) |
| 1963 | 1·8647** | 0·2019* | 0·8518** | (1·0537) | 0·93 | 203·81** | (0·079) |
| 1964 | 1·7358** | 0·1602 | 0·9306** | (1·0908) | 0·93 | 223·04** | (0·073) |
| 1965 | 1·8225** | 0·1854* | 0·8916** | (1·0770) | 0·94 | 257·83** | (0·098) |
| 1966 | 1·7132** | 0·1309 | 0·9655** | (1·0964)† | 0·94 | 254·08** | (0·075) |
| 1967 | 1·7661** | 0·1217 | 0·9680** | (1·0897)† | 0·94 | 255·18** | (0·057) |
| 1968 | 1·8283** | 0·1471 | 0·9468** | (1·0939)† | 0·94 | 254·66** | (0·075) |
| 1969 | 1·8398** | 0·1185 | 0·9787** | (1·0972)† | 0·94 | 263·33** | (0·070) |
| 1970 | 1·6998** | 0·2362* | 0·9080** | (1·1442)* | 0·93 | 208·92** | (0·209) |
| 1971 | 1·8502** | 0·0967 | 0·9998** | (1·0965)† | 0·93 | 216·30** | (0·047) |
| 1972 | 2·1135** | 0·3062* | 0·7532** | (1·0594) | 0·894 | 132·17** | (0·139) |

[a] See key to Table 5.1.

and $F$) is high in every year: $\bar{R}^2$ exceeded 0·9 and the $F$ statistic is significant at the 1 per cent level in every case, but the results are disappointing in several respects.

$A$ and $\beta$ are statistically significant at the 1 per cent level, but $\alpha$ is never significant at this level and only occasionally at the 5 per cent level. The zero-order correlation coefficients indicate that there exists strong multicollinearity between $K$ and $L$, implying that the reported estimates are individually unreliable. Comparison with the work of other authors suggests that $\alpha$ is smaller and $\beta$ larger than would have been expected, and in addition they are not stable over time.

The coefficients $\alpha$ and $\beta$ are individually unreliable, although their combined value $(\alpha + \beta)$ is unaffected by the problem of multicollinearity and provides a measure of industry-level returns to scale (with $\alpha + \beta > 1$ implying increasing, and $\alpha + \beta < 1$ implying decreasing, returns to scale). Increasing returns to scale characterise all of the functions: the combined coefficients are statistically greater than unity at the 10 per cent level of significance in a number of years and at the 5 per cent level in 1970. Increasing returns to scale appear to become greater in magnitude and statistically more significant towards the end of the sample period.

The technical efficiency parameter, $A$, is statistically different from zero at the 1 per cent level in all periods. However, the results reported in Table 7.1 give no indication of a simple growth path for $A$ over time. This can be contrasted with theoretical models, which often assume that the technical-efficiency parameter grows steadily (often exponentially) with time.

An obvious generalisation, which has been made by other authors, is to introduce hours. Until recently this was achieved by using labour hours as an explanatory variable,

$$Y_{jt} = A_t K_{jt}^{\alpha_t} (L_{jt} H_{jt})^{\beta_t} \tag{7.11}$$

but Feldstein (1967) and Craine (1972) have separated hours as an additional explanatory variable,

$$Y_{jt} = A_t K_{jt}^{\alpha_t} L_{jt}^{\beta_t} H_{jt}^{\gamma_t} \tag{7.12}$$

These two functional forms were estimated using the same data, but the results, which (as we might expect) show the same traits as those reported in Table 7.1, are not reported here. In particular, strong multicollinearity between $K$ and $L$ and between $K$ and $LH$ make the individual estimates of $\alpha$ and $\beta$ unreliable. The labour variable when weighted by hours still makes a significant contribution to the explanation of output, and the revised $\beta$ is of much the same size, and changes over time in much the same way, as previously. There is nothing in the results from equation (7.11) to indicate that they are an improvement on the results from (7.10). In the function where hours are distinguished separately, $H$ is not statistically significant, $\gamma$ is unstable and $A$ is even less tenable than before. Part of the explanation appears to be that average hours were roughly constant across industries and this makes the separate estimation of $A$ and $\gamma$ impossible.

A more important aspect of the results remains hidden in the main body of Table 7.1. It is associated with a problem that has received scant treatment in the literature on production functions. Equation (7.10) is mathematically identical to

$$\frac{Y_{jt}}{L_{jt}} = A_t \left( \frac{K_{jt}}{L_{jt}} \right)^{\alpha_t} L_{jt}^{(\alpha_t + \beta_t - 1)} \tag{7.13}$$

If the production function is estimated in this form, the coefficients $A$, $\alpha$ and $\beta$ are identical to those reported in Table 7.1, but the overall fit of the regression (again, measured by $\bar{R}^2$ and $F$) is very much lower. The final column of Table 7.1 reports the revised values of $\bar{R}^2$, which indicate that almost none of the variation in labour productivity across industries has been explained. Whilst labour productivity has a smaller variance across industries than output itself, the proportion of this variance explained by the Cobb–Douglas function has declined even more.

Griliches and Ringstad (1974, p. 64), when estimating Cobb–Douglas functions for a cross-section of Norwegian manufacturing establishments, discovered that this transformation reduced their $\bar{R}^2$ from 0·94 to 0·35. They argue that the transformation does not affect the real explanatory power of the model, which was quite low. The only way out of this dilemma appears to be to measure the fit when each of the possible alternative transformations is made. When a high explanatory power is obtained for all possible formulations, the overall fit of the model can be said to be good. Here we content ourselves with obtaining a high explanatory power for the labour-productivity form, but this in practice proves an extremely difficult task. This form has the advantage that it avoids the tendency of purely scale effects (i.e. large industries tend to employ large amounts of capital and labour) to swamp the effects of variations in labour and capital on the output of industries of a given size.

One obvious reason why little variation in labour productivity has been explained may be that the Cobb–Douglas function is too restrictive and a more general CES form is appropriate. The variables entering the function were centred on their geometric means (in the way suggested by Griliches and Ringstad) and the Kmenta CES form was then estimated:

$$\frac{Y_{jt}}{L_{jt}} = a_0 + a_1 \log L_{jt} + a_2 \log\left(\frac{K_{jt}}{L_{jt}}\right) + a_3 \left[\log\left(\frac{K_{jt}}{L_{jt}}\right)\right]^2 \qquad (7.14)$$

The results are reported in Table 7.2. In no sense were they satisfactory. The $\alpha$ coefficient ($a_2$) was significant only once at the 5 per cent level or better, although in six of the twelve cases it was significant at the 10 per cent level or better. Returns

Table 7.2

Annual CES production functions[a]

| Year | $a_0$ | $a_1$ | $a_2$ | $a_3$ | $\bar{R}^2$ | $F$ |
|------|-------|-------|-------|-------|-------------|-----|
| 1961 | 1·0284** | 0·0164 | 0·2029 | 0·0238 | – | 0·889 |
| 1962 | 1·0158** | 0·0248 | 0·1924 | 0·0601 | – | 0·942 |
| 1963 | 1·0077** | 0·0255 | 0·2375* | 0·1197 | – | 1·746 |
| 1964 | 1·0080** | 0·0693 | 0·1876† | 0·1085 | 0·066 | 1·727 |
| 1965 | 1·0326** | 0·0578 | 0·1781† | 0·0058 | 0·037 | 1·401 |
| 1966 | 1·0308** | 0·0778 | 0·1248 | 0·0164 | 0·015 | 1·1527 |
| 1967 | 1·0101** | 0·0671 | 0·1166 | 0·0923 | 0·013 | 1·1328 |
| 1968 | 1·0036** | 0·0753 | 0·1629† | 0·1192 | 0·061 | 1·6697 |
| 1969 | 1·0100** | 0·0750 | 0·1480 | 0·0975 | 0·035 | 1·3696 |
| 1970 | 0·9174** | 0·1473* | 0·3911** | 0·4161** | 0·440 | 9·0944** |
| 1971 | 0·9783** | 0·0878 | 0·1535 | 0·1921 | 0·071 | 1·7878 |
| 1972 | −0·0278 | 0·0621 | 0·3200* | 0·0678 | 0·136 | 2·6311* |

[a] See key to Table 5.1.

to scale ($a_1$) were significant only in 1970 and then only at the 5 per cent level. The second-order term ($a_3$) also was significant only in 1970, but in this case at the 1 per cent level. The general insignificance of $a_3$ gave little hope that it would yield sensible values for the elasticity of substitution. This in fact proved to be the case, with $\Phi < -1$ in seven of the 12 years and $\sigma$ highly unstable (varying from 1·0810 to 4·0966) in the remaining years. Even in the one case where $a_3$ was significant, $\Phi$ was less than $-1$. It is possible that the samples were not large enough and did not have sufficient variation of $K$ and $L$ to allow $a_3$ to be estimated with sufficient precision.

*Three-year pooled data*

The results reported so far suggest that further work on cross-sectional production functions based on data drawn from a single year would probably not be very rewarding.

A lack of variability in the data seems to be the cause of both multicollinearity between $K$ and $L$ and the lack of precision in estimating $a_3$. This may be avoided by pooling the cross-sectional and time-series dimensions of the data. It seemed most interesting to increase the sample size by the smallest amount necessary to reduce multicollinearity to acceptable levels. The cross-sectional data for three consecutive years were pooled, and in this way a moving pool of data was formed (1961–63, 1962–64, ..., 1970–72). This procedure still allows the paths of the estimated coefficients to be traced over time, but the coefficients are now averages over three years.

The results of estimating the basic Cobb–Douglas function described by equation (7.10) are reported in Table 7.3. The overall fit of the regressions measured by $\bar{R}^2$

Table 7.3

Three-year pooled Cobb–Douglas functions[a]

| Period | $A$ | $\alpha$ | $\beta$ | $(\alpha + \beta)$ | $\bar{R}^2$ | $F$ | $(\bar{R}^2)$ |
|---|---|---|---|---|---|---|---|
| 1961–63 | 1·8426** | 0·2258** | 0·8304** | (1·0562)† | 0·92 | 555·59** | 0·119 |
| 1962–64 | 1·8022** | 0·1957** | 0·8732** | (1·0689)* | 0·93 | 615·91** | 0·111 |
| 1963–65 | 1·8056** | 0·1837** | 0·8908** | (1·0745)** | 0·94 | 714·98** | 0·119 |
| 1964–66 | 1·7565** | 0·1598** | 0·9285** | (1·0883)** | 0·94 | 779·23** | 0·120 |
| 1965–67 | 1·7665** | 0·1470** | 0·9409** | (1·0816)** | 0·94 | 813·55** | 0·113 |
| 1966–68 | 1·7721** | 0·1400** | 0·9532** | (1·0932)** | 0·94 | 793·65** | 0·111 |
| 1967–69 | 1·8112** | 0·1356** | 0·9585** | (1·0941)** | 0·94 | 801·41** | 0·110 |
| 1968–70 | 1·7896** | 0·1780** | 0·9345** | (1·1125)** | 0·94 | 748·70** | 0·159 |
| 1969–71 | 1·8006** | 0·1554** | 0·9572** | (1·1126)** | 0·94 | 711·87** | 0·143 |
| 1970–72 | 1·8876** | 0·2084** | 0·8929** | (1·1013)** | 0·92 | 543·63** | 0·155 |

[a] See key to Table 5.1.

and $F$ again appears to be very good. In addition, the strength of the multicollinearity between capital and labour is diminished sufficiently to allow both $\alpha$ and $\beta$ to be significant at the 1 per cent level in all of the samples. Over the period 1961–69, $\alpha$ falls steadily while $\beta$ increases, but by the end of the period they return almost to their 1961–63 levels. As in the case of the annual results, other authors' works suggest that $\alpha$ is slightly smaller and $\beta$ slightly greater than might be expected. The estimated returns to scale are of the same order of magnitude as in the annual results. In all but two cases $(\alpha + \beta)$ is significantly greater than unity at the 1 per cent level and in the remaining cases it is significant at the 10 per cent and 5 per cent levels. The technical efficiency parameter still fails to grow steadily over time, although its value at the end of the period exceeds its initial value. As in the annual case, Table 7.3 again reports the $\bar{R}^2$ for the transformed function (see the extreme right-hand column). The $\bar{R}^2$ are somewhat higher than in the annual cases, but again do not achieve acceptable levels.

Table 7.4

Three-year pooled Cobb–Douglas functions with dummies[a]

| Period | $D_1$ | $D_2$ | $D_3$ | $\alpha$ | $\beta$ | $(\alpha + \beta)$ | $\bar{R}^2$ | $F$ | $(\bar{R}^2)$ |
|---|---|---|---|---|---|---|---|---|---|
| 1961–63 | 1·8302** | 1·8305** | 1·8624** | 0·2237** | 0·8326** | (1·0563)† | 0·921 | 272·51** | (0·102) |
| 1962–64 | 1·7616** | 1·7957** | 1·8444*** | 0·1931*** | 0·8757*** | (1·0688)* | 0·929 | 306·19** | (0·105) |
| 1963–65 | 1·7691** | 1·8177*** | 1·8344*** | 0·1821*** | 0·8919*** | (1·0740)* | 0·937 | 354·08** | (0·110) |
| 1964–66 | 1·7469** | 1·7645*** | 1·7595*** | 0·1591*** | 0·9290** | (1·0881)** | 0·941 | 381·58** | (0·101) |
| 1965–67 | 1·7608** | 1·7558*** | 1·7816*** | 0·1462** | 0·9417*** | (1·0879)*** | 0·944 | 398·86** | (0·095) |
| 1966–68 | 1·7279** | 1·7544*** | 1·8275*** | 0·1334* | 0·9598*** | (1·0932)** | 0·944 | 399·46*** | (0·115) |
| 1967–69 | 1·7517** | 1·8251** | 1·8575*** | 0·1292* | 0·9644*** | (1·0936) | 0·944 | 404·46** | (0·116) |
| 1968–70 | 1·7557** | 1·7868** | 1·8265*** | 0·1739*** | 0·9384*** | (1·1123) | 0·940 | 370·79** | (0·151) |
| 1969–71 | 1·7814** | 1·8227** | 1·7965*** | 0·1535*** | 0·9590*** | (1·1125) | 0·936 | 349·66** | (0·128) |
| 1970–72 | 1·8745** | 1·8549** | 1·9205*** | 0·2079*** | 0·8943*** | (1·1022) | 0·920 | 272·69** | (0·143) |

[a] See key to Table 5.1.

The introduction of hours had almost exactly the same consequences as in the annual regressions and the results are not therefore reported in detail. An alternative generalisation is to allow the $A$ parameter to change from year to year. The results for the simplest Cobb–Douglas function are reported in Table 7.4. The function was estimated using two dummies and a constant, but translated into a form with three dummies (and no overall constant). The results are almost identical to those reported in Table 7.3, with the size and significance of $\alpha$ and $\beta$ similar to in the previous estimates. The explanatory power for the basic formulations was basically the same in both tables, but for the transformed functions it was slightly lower in Table 7.4. The dummy variables, however, did not increase from sample to sample. They showed a tendency to increase within any particular sample, but in no case were the second- and third-year dummies significantly different from an overall constant. For completeness, hours were included along with the time dummies, in the alternative ways already described. The results were, however, almost identical to those described earlier and are therefore not reported in detail.

Table 7.5

Three-year pooled CES functions[a]

| Period | $a_0$ | $a_1$ | $a_2$ | $a_3$ | $\bar{R}^2$ | $F$ |
|---|---|---|---|---|---|---|
| 1961–63 | −0·0159 | 0·0450 | 0·2371** | 0·0755 | 0·116 | 4·21** |
| 1962–64 | −0·0304 | 0·0647* | 0·2197** | 0·0959 | 0·120 | 5·28** |
| 1963–65 | −0·0203 | 0·0717* | 0·2022** | 0·0744 | 0·124 | 5·46** |
| 1964–66 | −0·0144 | 0·0871** | 0·1675** | 0·0387 | 0·114 | 5·07** |
| 1965–67 | −0·0078 | 0·0873** | 0·1509** | 0·0290 | 0·105 | 4·73** |
| 1966–68 | −0·0192 | 0·0915** | 0·1480** | 0·0702 | 0·113 | 5·02** |
| 1967–69 | −0·0255 | 0·0915** | 0·1484** | 0·0922 | 0·120 | 5·33** |
| 1968–70 | −0·0522† | 0·1041** | 0·1952** | 0·1701** | 0·225 | 10·19** |
| 1969–71 | −0·0631† | 0·1075** | 0·1887** | 0·1901** | 0·233 | 10·60** |
| 1970–72 | −0·0611† | 0·1016** | 0·3180** | 0·1816** | 0·214 | 9·61** |

[a] See key to Table 5.1.

The larger size of the sample (now approximately 96 observations) appears to have significantly reduced the problem of multicollinearity between capital and labour. There is now reason to believe that if the second-order terms of the CES function are important, then $a_3$ in the Kmenta form should now be found to be significantly different from zero. The results of estimating the Kmenta form on the pooled information are reported in Table 7.5. The returns-to-scale term, $a_1$, is almost always significant at the 5 per cent level or better. The coefficient $a_2$ (which is capital's share weighted by the returns to scale, $\theta b$) is significant at the 1 per cent level in every case. The key coefficient in the Kmenta form, $a_3$, is generally insignificantly different from zero, and in the cases where it is significant it is associated with values of $\Phi$ less than $-1$. The estimated value of $\sigma$ is almost always unacceptable.

Table 7.6

Twelve-year pooled Cobb–Douglas functions[a]

| Regression:<br>Functional form: | (1)<br>$Y = AK^\alpha L^\beta$ | (2)<br>$Y = AK^\alpha(LH)^\beta$ | (3)<br>$Y = AK^\alpha L^\beta H^\gamma$ | (4)<br>$Y = D_t K^\alpha L^\beta$ | (5)<br>$Y = D_t K^\alpha(LH)^\beta$ | (6)<br>$Y = D_t K^\alpha L^\beta H^\gamma$ |
|---|---|---|---|---|---|---|
| $A$ | 1·8244** | -1·4464** | 5·4365** | | | |
| $D_1$ | | | | 1·6744** | -1·8131** | 1·4391** |
| $D_2$ | | | | 1·6766** | -1·7978** | 1·4426** |
| $D_3$ | | | | 1·7122** | -1·7860** | 1·4621** |
| $D_4$ | | | | 1·7606** | -1·7387** | 1·5114** |
| $D_5$ | | | | 1·7772** | -1·6985** | 1·5319** |
| $D_6$ | | | | 1·7965** | -1·6847** | 1·5311** |
| $D_7$ | | | | 1·8664** | -1·6482** | 1·5556** |
| $D_8$ | | | | 1·8974** | -1·5997** | 1·6243** |
| $D_9$ | | | | 1·9355** | -1·5666** | 1·6554** |
| $D_{10}$ | | | | 1·9131** | -1·4955** | 1·7153** |
| $D_{11}$ | | | | 1·9696** | -1·4993** | 1·6814** |
| $D_{12}$ | | | | | -1·4501** | 1·7426** |
| $\alpha$ | 0·2117** | 0·2050** | 0·2045** | 0·1807** | 0·1600** | 0·1666** |
| $\beta$ | 0·8751** | 0·8764** | 0·8953** | 0·9063** | 0·9212** | 0·9231** |
| $(\alpha + \beta)$ | (1·0868)** | (1·0814)** | (1·0998)** | (1·0870)** | (1·0812)** | (1·0897)** |
| $\gamma$ | | | -0·9763** | | | 0·0569 |
| $\bar{R}^2$ | 0·926 | 0·926 | 0·930 | 0·931 | 0·934 | 0·934 |
| $F$ | 2375·15** | 2244·53** | 1623·63** | 399·15** | 374·71** | 399·08** |
| $(\bar{R}^2)$ | (0·147) | (0·132) | (0·161) | (0·213) | (0·191) | (0·233) |

[a] See key to Table 5.1.

It seems an obvious step to pool all of the data (32 MLHs for 12 years) and obtain average values of $\alpha$ and $\beta$ over the whole period. The results obtained are reported in Table 7.6. Regression (1) is the simplest Cobb–Douglas function. The values taken by $A$, $\alpha$ and $\beta$ are broadly consistent with those found using the smaller (three-year) pools, and there are significant increasing returns to scale at the 1 per cent level. The Cobb–Douglas function was re-estimated including a different dummy variable in each year and appears as regression (4). This innovation changed the values of $\alpha$ and $\beta$ only slightly, and all of the estimated coefficients are significantly different from zero at the 1 per cent level. The $\alpha$ coefficient was slightly smaller and $\beta$ slightly larger when the dummies were included, but the returns to scale were almost unchanged. The individual dummies were all significantly different from zero, and those for later years became significantly different from the 1961 value by 1967. The role played by hours in the Cobb–Douglas function is illustrated by regressions (2), (3), (5) and (6). In both forms in which hours can be introduced they have the effect of reducing $\alpha$ and raising $\beta$ slightly, although both remain significant at the 1 per cent level. Weighting the labour variable by the number of hours worked does not alter the overall explanatory power of the model. This is also true where hours appear as a separate explanatory variable: $\gamma$ has the wrong sign in regression (3) and it is not significant when industry dummies are introduced. The explanatory power of the transformed functions (labour-productivity form), when measured by $\bar{R}^2$ and $F$, remains extremely low.

One interesting point is that the technical efficiency parameters, $D_t$, now show a strong upward trend over time ($t = 1, \ldots, 12$). In the Cobb–Douglas function described by regression (4), $D$ rises by 17·63 per cent over the 12 year period. The minor downturns are associated with years of recession in the engineering industry: they may be a consequence of mismeasuring input usage or they may be a feature of technical change (for example, the result of failing to invest sufficient to overcome depreciation).

## Inter-industry variations in labour productivity: some insights

Engineering forms a much more homogeneous sample than has been used by most researchers in the past. Shipbuilding and motor vehicles, for example, have features that make it natural to include them within engineering. Nevertheless, the engineering group is composed of a number of diverse elements: shipbuilding and electronics produce technically distinct products and require different mixes of capital types and labour skills to produce them. An obvious reaction, therefore, is to look at more detailed subgroups of engineering and to investigate whether the CES functions now perform any better. The study concentrates on the Cobb–Douglas function, the results of which are sufficient to illustrate the conclusions drawn in this chapter.

Engineering is subdivided into mechanical, electrical, vehicles and metal goods not elsewhere specified. Tables 7.7–7.10 report results for the basic Cobb–Douglas function for each of these industries in turn, based on the three-year pools of information. Several important conclusions can be drawn. First, in absolute form all the functions appear to perform well: $\bar{R}^2$ exceeds 0·9 in all of the samples and $F$ is significant at the 1 per cent level in every case. Second, the smaller sample sizes cause the problem of multicollinearity between $K$ and $L$ to reappear. Only mechanical engineering, which has the greatest number of observations, appears to be largely untouched by this problem. The values of $\alpha$ and $\beta$ for this industry subgroup are quite different from those calculated for all engineering. Third, there is some evidence to suggest considerable differences between industries in the returns to scale experienced. Vehicles are characterised by significant increasing returns to scale, while both electrical and metal goods not elsewhere specified show some signs of decreasing returns to scale. Finally, although the results for the all-years pooled data are not reported in detail, they show considerable differences in the rates of improvement in technical efficiency.

The overall fit of the function varies considerably. This can most clearly be seen in the form where labour productivity is the dependent variable. The final column of each table reports $\bar{R}^2$ for the transformed functions. In the case of vehicles, the basic Cobb–Douglas function is almost as good at explaining variations in labour productivity as it is at explaining variations in output. Mechanical engineering shows a similar although not so marked improvement. The results for electrical engineering and metal goods not elsewhere specified are by no means as good, although for some periods there is an improvement over the results for all engineering.

One interpretation of the results is that vehicles and mechanical engineering form samples within which the technology of production is common across MLHs and Cobb–Douglas in form. There is good reason to believe that metal goods not elsewhere specified is a rag-bag of industries that are grouped together not because they have anything in common, but because they have nothing to link them with another engineering group. The case of electrical engineering is much less obvious. While it embraces a diverse collection of MLHs, ranging from one-off heavy electrical capital goods to mass-produced consumer goods, this is to some extent also true of mechanical engineering. This interpretation of the improved results must be treated with caution. It becomes difficult to decide whether it is the more homogeneous technologies, or simply the lower degree of variability in the sample, that causes the improved empirical performance.

Neoclassical functions fail to provide an explanation of variations in productivity across the broad spectrum of engineering industries. They may, although the evidence is by no means conclusive, be relevant to more tightly defined industry subgroups. Capital and labour play a part in the explanation of inter-industry variations in labour productivity, but they do not by themselves tell the whole story. The problem of isolating other relevant variables is not wholly resolved here, although a number of 'quality' or 'performance' variables are tested. Not all of

Table 7.7

Three-year pooled: mechanical engineering[a]

| Period | $D_1$ | $D_2$ | $D_3$ | $\alpha$ | $\beta$ | $(\alpha + \beta)$ | $\bar{R}^2$ | $F$ | $(\bar{R}^2)$ |
|---|---|---|---|---|---|---|---|---|---|
| 1961–63 | 2·1508** | 2·1126** | 2·1390** | 0·6930** | 0·3700** | (1·0631) | 0·914 | 85·90** | (0·454) |
| 1962–64 | 2·0429** | 2·0717** | 2·1677** | 0·6694** | 0·4063** | (1·0757) | 0·930 | 106·88** | (0·495) |
| 1963–65 | 2·1168** | 2·1168** | 2·2140** | 0·6826** | 0·3842** | (1·0668) | 0·948 | 146·70** | (0·565) |
| 1964–66 | 2·0570** | 2·0013** | 2·0038** | 0·6869** | 0·4163** | (1·1032) | 0·949 | 150·17** | (0·562) |
| 1965–67 | 1·9646** | 1·9668** | 1·9431** | 0·6929** | 0·4193** | (1·1122)* | 0·958 | 182·62** | (0·613) |
| 1966–68 | 1·9493** | 1·9248** | 1·9424** | 0·7079** | 0·4101** | (1·1180)** | 0·967 | 233·48** | (0·696) |
| 1967–69 | 2·0441** | 2·0628** | 2·1237** | 0·6824** | 0·4060** | (1·0884)* | 0·966 | 229·30** | (0·699) |
| 1968–70 | 2·1847** | 2·2477** | 2·2586** | 0·6050** | 0·4488** | (1·0538) | 0·953 | 163·96** | (0·627) |
| 1969–71 | 2·2475** | 2·2649** | 2·2603** | 0·5127** | 0·5335** | (1·0462) | 0·934 | 114·98** | (0·498) |
| 1970–72 | 2·3395** | 2·3241** | 2·4009** | 0·3957** | 0·6257** | (1·0228) | 0·909 | 81·16** | (0·373) |

[a] See key to Table 5.1.

Table 7.8

Three-year pooled: electrical engineering[a]

| Period | $D_1$ | $D_2$ | $D_3$ | $\alpha$ | $\beta$ | $(\alpha + \beta)$ | $\bar{R}^2$ | $F$ | $(\bar{R}^2)$ |
|---|---|---|---|---|---|---|---|---|---|
| 1961–63 | 2·4113** | 2·4535** | 2·5017** | 0·0006 | 0·9169** | (0·9175) | 0·950 | 80·96** | (0·001) |
| 1962–64 | 2·6020** | 2·6514** | 2·6946** | −0·0210 | 0·9053** | (0·8843)† | 0·958 | 97·30** | (0·113) |
| 1963–65 | 2·7099** | 2·7537** | 2·7598** | −0·0022 | 0·8760** | (0·8738)* | 0·966 | 120·10** | (0·269) |
| 1964–66 | 2·6478** | 2·6536** | 2·6961** | 0·0046 | 0·8917** | (0·8963) | 0·965 | 117·69** | (0·172) |
| 1965–67 | 2·6813** | 2·7242** | 2·8016** | −0·0103 | 0·9000** | (0·8897) | 0·947 | 77·51** | (0·118) |
| 1966–68 | 2·7874** | 2·8667** | 2·9430** | −0·0558 | 0·9284** | (0·8726) | 0·941 | 69·04** | (0·073) |
| 1967–69 | 2·9000** | 2·9763** | 3·0285** | −0·0690 | 0·9338** | (0·8648) | 0·950 | 82·12** | (0·045) |
| 1968–70 | 3·0251** | 3·0778** | 3·1233** | −0·0860 | 0·9395** | (0·8535)† | 0·961 | 106·67** | (0·060) |
| 1969–71 | 3·2696** | 3·3164** | 3·3617** | −0·1240* | 0·9353** | (0·8113)* | 0·960 | 102·60** | (0·176) |
| 1970–72 | 3·1679** | 3·2147** | 3·3368** | −0·1127† | 0·9555** | (0·8428)† | 0·956 | 92·49** | (0·265) |

[a] See key to Table 5.1.

Table 7.9

Three-year pooled: vehicles[a]

| Period | $D_1$ | $D_2$ | $D_3$ | $\alpha$ | $\beta$ | $(\alpha + \beta)$ | $\bar{R}^2$ | $F$ | $(\bar{R}^2)$ |
|---|---|---|---|---|---|---|---|---|---|
| 1961–63 | 0·8862** | 0·8740** | 0·8556** | 0·5692** | 0·6718** | (1·2410)** | 0·990 | 353·52** | (0·869) |
| 1962–64 | 0·8300** | 0·8117** | 0·8293** | 0·5830** | 0·6682** | (1·2512)** | 0·993 | 476·36** | (0·903) |
| 1963–65 | 0·7769** | 0·8025** | 0·9143** | 0·5010** | 0·7533** | (1·2543)** | 0·992 | 450·07** | (0·889) |
| 1964–66 | 0·7074** | 0·8320** | 0·7803** | 0·3469** | 0·9231** | (1·2700)** | 0·993 | 512·20** | (0·884) |
| 1965–67 | 0·8249** | 0·7820** | 0·8025** | 0·1247 | 1·1431** | (1·2678)** | 0·996 | 882·32** | (0·919) |
| 1966–68 | 0·7591** | 0·7808** | 0·9012** | 0·1421 | 1·1918** | (1·2724)** | 0·997 | 1027·04** | (0·932) |
| 1967–69 | 0·8572** | 0·9842** | 1·0070** | 0·0071 | 1·2479** | (1·2550)** | 0·996 | 982·69** | (0·921) |
| 1968–70 | 0·8571** | 0·8749** | 1·0762** | 0·3939* | 0·8819** | (1·2758)** | 0·981 | 181·30** | (0·744) |
| 1969–71 | 0·9661** | 1·1587** | 0·9900** | 0·4064* | 0·8479** | (1·2543)** | 0·980 | 174·79** | (0·718) |
| 1970–72 | 1·4095** | 1·2310** | 1·4032** | 0·3229† | 0·8769** | (1·1998)** | 0·975 | 138·81** | (0·597) |

[a] See key to Table 5.1.

113

Table 7.10

Three-year pooled: metal goods not elsewhere specified[a]

| Period | $D_1$ | $D_2$ | $D_3$ | $\alpha$ | $\beta$ | $(\alpha+\beta)$ | $\bar{R}^2$ | $F$ | $(\bar{R}^2)$ |
|---|---|---|---|---|---|---|---|---|---|
| 1961–63 | 2·5764** | 2·5764** | 2·5894** | 0·2773 | 0·6023** | (0·8796) | 0·903 | 42·76 | (0·006) |
| 1962–64 | 2·4988*** | 2·4974*** | 2·5475*** | 0·2766 | 0·6278** | (0·9044) | 0·920 | 55·58 | (0·006) |
| 1963–65 | 2·4330** | 2·4824*** | 2·5154*** | 0·2645 | 0·6565** | (0·9210) | 0·928 | 65·69 | ( – ) |
| 1964–66 | 2·4880** | 2·5216** | 2·5066** | 0·2481 | 0·6703** | (0·9184) | 0·933 | 70·92 | ( – ) |
| 1965–67 | 2·6313*** | 2·6167** | 2·6300** | 0·2593 | 0·6307*** | (0·8900)† | 0·936 | 74·14 | (0·067) |
| 1966–68 | 2·6550*** | 2·6672*** | 2·7313*** | 0·2940† | 0·5881*** | (0·8821)* | 0·950 | 95·03 | (0·203) |
| 1967–69 | 2·6459*** | 2·7073*** | 2·6819*** | 0·3493* | 0·5421** | (0·8914)* | 0·952 | 101·05 | (0·208) |
| 1968–70 | 2·5657*** | 2·5434*** | 2·4699** | 0·2741† | 0·6518*** | (0·9259) | 0·957 | 111·62 | (0·086) |
| 1969–71 | 2·4687*** | 2·3940*** | 2·4015*** | 0·1473 | 0·7940*** | (0·9413) | 0·950 | 96·10 | ( – ) |
| 1970–72 | 2·6106*** | 2·6325*** | 2·2542** | 0·3908* | 0·5019*** | (0·8927) | 0·898 | 45·17 | (0·211) |

[a] See key to Table 5.1.

these fit neatly into a neoclassical world (the average ages of capital and labour, output growth and recent investment activity); some relate to aspects of the technology that have been given scant attention in the literature (shiftworking, establishment and firm size); and others (the degree of foreign-controlled operations, and the levels of concentration, specialisation and exclusiveness) relate more to market structure and industrial performance than to the technology of production.

The inclusion of 'quality' variables gives rise to additional problems of measurement, aggregation and specification. While some of the problems are touched on briefly, a heroic stance is adopted. Only in Chapter 8 is an attempt made to develop a model of firm equilibrium where such variables appear less out of place. The functions reported here are modifications of the basic Cobb–Douglas form

$$\frac{Y}{L} = A \left(\frac{K}{L}\right)^{\alpha} L^{(\alpha+\beta-1)} \prod_{l} \rho_l Q_l u \qquad (7.15)$$

where $Q_1, \ldots, Q_{11}$ represent respectively: the average age of capital; average age of labour; percentage of employees working shifts; establishment size; firm size; percentage of sales by foreign-controlled firms; five-firm concentration ratio; specialisation ratio; exclusiveness ratio; recent growth performance; and recent investment activity.

Information of the type required here is generally available only from the *Census of Production*. The estimates reported therefore relate to two annual cross-sections, 1963 and 1968. Only the data on shiftworking and the averages ages of capital and labour are from other sources and refer to different points in time. Shiftworking data are available for the years 1964 and 1968 from the *Ministry of Labour Gazette* and the *New Earnings Survey*, respectively. Average-age data are published for 1961, 1966 and 1971; data about the age of capital are from the *Census of Metal Working Machine Tools*, and information about the age of labour is from the *Census of Population*. The shiftworking data were left unchanged, as the years to which they related coincided reasonably well with those of the quinquennial censuses, but the average-age data were interpolated linearly to provide estimates for the census years.

Given the basic theme of the study, it seemed interesting to focus on three variables: the average age of capital, recent output growth, and investment activity. All three variables can be given a vintage interpretation. Older capital, for example, will tend to be less efficient and associated with lower levels of labour productivity. The average age of capital is associated with important problems of measurement: its construction, which follows the work of Bacon and Eltis (1974), is based on stringent assumptions (for instance, a constant rate of growth in investment), which are made necessary by the data constraints; the data relates only to machine tools; and a given average age may be associated with various distributions of ages, which will have different average efficiencies of capital. The output-growth variable is linked with the vintage approach in the way described in Chapter 3. In this study the growth phenomenon is assumed to be symmetrical around $\Delta Y / Y = 0$ and thus $|\Delta Y / Y|$ is selected as the explanatory variable where the change is calculated over the five years preceding each census ($\Delta Y_{63-58}/Y_{58}$ and $\Delta Y_{68-63}/Y_{63}$). In a similar way, the recent-investment-activity variable is constructed as the cumulative sum of net investment over the previous five years, deflated by the amount of fuel consumed in the census year ($\sum_{t=58}^{63} IN_t/F_{63}$ and $\sum_{t=63}^{68} IN_t/F_{68}$). The variable represents an attempt to measure the amount of investment activity relative to the existing capital stock.

These variables were initially treated as alternative measures of the same pheno-menon, and the results are reported in Table 7.11. Although a great deal of the

Table 7.11

Quality variables[a]

| Regression | | $A$ | $\alpha$ | $\alpha+\beta-1$ | $\rho$ | $\bar{R}^2$ | $F$ |
|---|---|---|---|---|---|---|---|
| 1963 | (1) | 3·4285* | 0·1937† | 0·0510 | −0·6024 | 0·074 | 1·80 |
| | (2) | 1·2470** | 0·1968* | 0·0622 | 0·1659** | 0·275 | 4·92** |
| | (3) | 2·7534** | 0·0656 | −0·3622 | 0·3897** | 0·400 | 7·43** |
| 1968 | (1) | 4·0386** | 0·1640 | 0·0867† | −0·8429 | 0·115 | 2·30 |
| | (2) | 1·4220** | 0·1928 | 0·0797 | 0·1321 | 0·118 | 2·38 |
| | (3) | 2·5058** | 0·0590 | −0·2844* | 0·3671** | 0·267 | 4·53** |

[a] See key to Table 5.1.

variation in labour productivity is left to be explained, a vintage effect does appear to exist. The average-age variable, regression (1) in Table 7.11, has the expected sign (i.e. older vintages are less efficient) and comes close to being significant in 1968, for which a slightly more reliable measure of age was available; but the additional variable does not radically change the overall fit of the function. Regressions (2) and (3), where $\rho$ relates to output growth and investment activity respectively, show a

Table 7.12

The explanation of labour productivity:

| Regression | | $A$ | $\alpha$ | $\alpha+\beta-1$ | $\rho_1$ | $\rho_2$ | $\rho_3$ | $\rho_4$ |
|---|---|---|---|---|---|---|---|---|
| 1963 | (1) | 0·2692 | 0·0697 | −0·3012 | −0·6652 | 1·3340 | −0·0214 | 0·2519 |
| | (2) | −5·1789 | 0·1004 | 0·0207 | −0·8057 | 3·0571 | 0·0995 | −0·0841 |
| | (3) | −7·8722 | 0·1023 | 0·0408 | – | 3·0648* | 0·0931 | 0·0611 |
| | (4) | 4·0042 | 0·0559 | −0·2868 | – | −0·1335 | 0·0284 | 0·1677 |
| 1968 | (1) | −14·4212* | 0·3336** | 0·1524** | 0·9101 | 0·6389 | 0·3974** | −1·4342** |
| | (2) | −5·2432 | 0·1495 | 0·0509 | −0·4136 | 1·3013 | 0·2692† | −0·6957* |
| | (3) | −9·2783† | 0·2584** | 0·0078 | – | 1·1556 | 0·3098** | −1·0477** |
| | (4) | −4·6757 | 0·1418 | 0·0064 | – | 0·8981 | 0·2767** | −0·7274* |

[a] See key to Table 5.1.

considerable improvement: $\bar{R}^2$ is higher and the $F$ statistic is significant at the 1 per cent level in three of the four cases.

Regressions (1) in Table 7.12 show the impact of the eleven 'quality' variables when they all appear together. The overall fit of the function improves on the results reported in Table 7.11 in both years, although the function performs better in 1968 than in 1963. $\bar{R}^2$ is higher in 1963 than in the case discussed earlier, but the $F$ statistic is significant only at the 5 per cent level. In 1968, however, five of the eleven 'quality' variables are significant at the 1 per cent level and one at the 5 per cent level, while $\bar{R}^2$ reaches the respectable figure of 0·594 and $F$ is significant at the 1 per cent level. The general significance of these variables in 1968 can be contrasted with the results obtained by Griliches and Ringstad (1971).

It was suggested earlier that the average-age-of-capital, output-growth and investment-activity variables are alternative summary measures of any vintage effects. Treating them as alternatives, regressions (2), (3) and (4) adopt the average age of capital, output growth and investment activity, respectively, as the summary variables (and in each case exclude the other two alternatives). The effect in every case is to lower $\bar{R}^2$, and the $F$ statistic is significant only in regressions (3), where the output-growth variable appears. The significance of the estimated coefficients are otherwise very similar to those described above. The output-growth variable appears to play an extremely important part in explaining cross-industry variations in labour productivity.

The most striking difference between the results for 1963 and those for 1968 is the general significance of the coefficients in 1968, as against their insignificance in 1963. While the overall fit of the functions is slightly better in 1968 than in 1963, there is no radical difference. Part of the explanation must therefore lie with the higher levels of multicollinearity and the slightly smaller sample size in 1963. A further explanation, which is taken up in more detail in Chapter 8 and requires much more intensive empirical testing, is that the significance of the variables varies over the trade cycle. In boom years (1963, for example), the market-structure and industry-

quality and performance variables[a]

| $\rho_5$ | $\rho_6$ | $\rho_7$ | $\rho_8$ | $\rho_9$ | $\rho_{10}$ | $\rho_{11}$ | $\bar{R}^2$ | $F$ |
|---|---|---|---|---|---|---|---|---|
| −0·2776 | 0·0148 | −0·1346 | −0·9169 | 0·8006 | 0·1314† | 0·3407 | 0·416 | 2·53* |
| 0·0350 | 0·0878† | −0·3121 | −1·1507 | 0·9593 | − | | 0·220 | 1·72 |
| −0·0863 | 0·0606 | −0·2348 | −0·6876 | 0·4190 | 0·1544* | | 0·375 | 2·52* |
| −0·2211 | 0·0376 | −0·0179 | −0·5364 | 0·3686 | − | 0·3388 | 0·270 | 1·94 |
| 1·2468** | 0·0916** | −0·0010 | 2·1452* | 0·0088 | 0·3854** | −0·1819 | 0·594 | 4·37** |
| 0·5873* | 0·0729† | 0·0435 | 0·6678 | −0·0440 | − | | 0·262 | 1·97 |
| 0·9180** | 0·0658* | −0·0009 | 1·3160† | −0·0510 | 0·2615** | | 0·544 | 4·25** |
| 0·6023* | 0·0750† | 0·0453 | 0·5804 | 0·0302 | − | 0·0507 | 0·251 | 1·91 |

## Table 7.13

Zero-order correlation coefficients: quality and performance variables

| | Average age of capital | Average age of labour | Percentage working shifts | Establishment size | Firm size | Percentage of sales by foreign-controlled firms | Five-firm concentration ratio | Specialisation ratio | Exclusiveness ratio | Output-growth activity |
|---|---|---|---|---|---|---|---|---|---|---|
| Average age of labour | 0·573 | | | | | | | | | |
| Percentage working shifts | 0·067 | 0·273 | | | | | | | | |
| Establishment size | 0·306 | 0·084 | 0·143 | | | | | | | |
| Firm size | 0·252 | 0·053 | 0·094 | 0·982 | | | | | | |
| Percentage of sales by foreign-controlled firms | −0·491 | −0·604 | −0·207 | −0·133 | −0·116 | | | | | |
| Five-firm concentration ratio | 0·192 | 0·274 | 0·343 | 0·561 | 0·558 | −0·212 | | | | |
| Specialisation ratio | −0·014 | 0·267 | 0·246 | −0·189 | −0·192 | −0·407 | 0·019 | | | |
| Exclusiveness ratio | −0·123 | −0·087 | −0·141 | 0·184 | 0·178 | −0·086 | 0·205 | 0·413 | | |
| Output-growth activity | −0·485 | −0·304 | −0·176 | −0·163 | −0·178 | 0·388 | −0·231 | −0·313 | −0·146 | |
| Investment activity | −0·223 | −0·060 | 0·155 | 0·021 | 0·080 | 0·096 | −0·016 | 0·186 | −0·035 | 0·280 |

performance variables may play a relatively small role, but in times of recession (such as 1968) they may become much more important.

Exploring the results for 1968 in slightly more detail reveals that capital and labour both play a significant part in explaining variations in labour productivity. The coefficient on the average age of capital had an unexpected positive sign, but was insignificantly different from zero. The average age of workers did not make a significant contribution, although older, more experienced workers were associated with higher levels of productivity. $\rho_3$ was significant at the 1 per cent level, indicating that greater shiftworking was associated with higher labour productivity. Although firm and establishment size were multicollinear, $\rho_3$ and $\rho_4$ were both significantly different from zero. The signs indicated that smaller establishments but larger firms were associated with higher levels of productivity. Industries with higher percentages of foreign-controlled firms were significantly more efficient. Higher levels of concentration (based on a five-firm concentration ratio) were associated with lower levels of productivity, but not significantly so. Coefficient $\rho_8$, associated with the degree of specialisation, was significant at the 5 per cent level with the expected sign, while $\rho_9$, associated with the degree of exclusiveness, was insignificant. The output-growth variable was significant with the expected sign, but the investment-activity variable made an insignificant contribution and had the wrong sign.

For completeness, Table 7.13 gives the zero-order correlation coefficients for 1968. While space is not available to discuss them in detail, a number of the correlations appear extremely interesting (i.e. between the average age of capital and the other variables).

## Conclusions

Though a great deal more research needs to be done, the results presented in this chapter enable a number of important conclusions to be drawn. First, while the basic CES functions give every appearance of performing well when explaining inter-industry variations in the level of output, they give an entirely different impression when explaining labour productivity. Second, while the performance of the basic functions can be improved by estimating them separately for more tightly defined industry subgroups, it is impossible to tell whether this is the result of greater similarities of technology or simply because of the reduction in the variability of the sample. Finally, it is suggested that, while there is a need for much more theoretical and empirical work, a more broadly based explanation of variations in productivity (which calls on 'quality' and 'performance' variables) is required. Chapter 8 is seen as a prelude to such a theory.

## Notes

[1] Some provisional estimates for this industry were reported in Bosworth

(1974b, pp. 153–96), but the data have been improved since this study was under-taken.

[2] It is easy to illustrate this point. A search involving 11 values of $\Phi$ with only three of $\theta$ involves 33 regressions for each sample. With 12 different samples, this is a total of 396 regressions. This method of 'search over a grid' has been used by Griliches and Ringstad (1971, pp. 79–80).

# 8   Neoclassical production functions: fact or fantasy?

## Introduction

Economic theory has for some time been living with an important contradiction arising out of the debate about the existence of aggregate neoclassical production functions. In recent years the neoclassicist has been forced increasingly on the defensive. The unfavourable result of the debate about problems of aggregation has caused him to retreat towards micro economics, and the absurdity of the assumption that capital is instantaneously and costlessly malleable has resulted in his interpreting observed points 'as if' they were drawn from a neoclassical world, an assumption that so far lacks justification. [1] At the same time, however, aggregate neoclassical production functions continue to be accepted as a statistically accurate description of observed points in the input–output space. The inconsistency between intuitive plausibility and empirical fact forms the subject of this chapter.

In order not to cast the net too widely, a secondary problem concerning variations in the results of neoclassical studies is avoided as far as possible. The body of empirical evidence has become sufficiently large in recent years to show that different types of data produce different results. Brown (1966, pp. 129–30), for example, has noted that the elasticity of substitution between inputs centres around the value of one-half in time-series studies, while it is closer to unity in cross-sectional work. Both Brown and Johansen (1972) have concluded that different relationships were being investigated in the two cases. Our attention focuses on the cross-sectional case, where the Cobb–Douglas (1928) function is by far the most consistent performer.

One can visualise the neoclassicists' reasons for entering the realms of micro theory. If an 'as if' explanation of neoclassical production functions could have been provided at the micro level, it might have been possible to aggregate and produce production functions consistent with those arising from the empirical studies. The neoclassicists, however, have found no explanation of the Cobb–Douglas phenomenon. The 'as if' defence, using a surrogate production function, has been discredited even at the micro level with the realisation of the relevance of the reswitching and reversing phenomena. Even had they been able to find such a justification at the micro level, they would have had to face the problem that the conditions of aggregation are generally so severe as to make the existence of the aggregate Cobb–Douglas function extremely unlikely. In the rush to find safer

121

ground, the Cobb–Douglas function has been abandoned, even though it continues to yield 'good' empirical results (see Solow, 1966, pp. 1259–60). We are left to look at this relic of bygone days and wonder what hypothesis, if any, is being tested (see Blaug, 1974, p. 18).

A review of the explanations of the Cobb–Douglas relationship is provided in the next section. There can be little doubt that the existing explanations do not give the whole story. The third section of this chapter attempts to provide an alternative avenue of thought combining the more important of the existing explanations. The final section draws some conclusions about how we can interpret the aggregate Cobb–Douglas function.


## A review of the literature

The literature explaining the aggregate Cobb–Douglas result can be divided into three broad groups. First, some economists have regarded the relationship as an 'empirical law' in its own right. Second, a number of economists have argued that, although the underlying technology of production may not be Cobb–Douglas, observations drawn from the real world behave 'as if' they are consistent with a neoclassical technology. Finally, it has been argued that the aggregate Cobb–Douglas function arises from features of the data that have little or nothing to do with the underlying technology of production.

### 'Empirical laws' and heroic aggregation

It was the neoclassicists' hope that the aggregate production function would prove a reflection of the underlying micro technologies. It is at a micro level, for example, that the economist would be more at ease talking about homogeneous capital and labour inputs. The immediate question was whether micro Cobb–Douglas technologies could be easily aggregated to the sort of functions estimated in the literature.

In reviewing the conclusions of the debate about problems of aggregation, we can kill two birds with one stone by moving into a vintage world. It has already been noted that vintage models are intuitively more appealing than are their neoclassical counterparts. A number of them (though by no means all) have assumed the existence of *ex ante* substitution possibilities in accord with neoclassical principles, and there is some hope that an aggregate production function may, in some way, reflect these underlying technologies. The simplest of these cases involves a putty–putty model of the Solow (1960) and Phelps (1962) variety. Allen (1968, pp. 283–6) investigates this type of model and assumes each *ex ante* function is Cobb–Douglas.

$$Y_{vt} = A^{gv}K_v^{\alpha}L_{vt}^{1-\alpha} \tag{8.1}$$

where $Y$, $K$ and $L$ denote output, capital and labour, respectively; and where $v$ denotes the $v$th vintage and $t$ the $t$th time period, where $t > v$.

The model is consistent with Solow neutral technical progress at a rate $g/\alpha$ up to the time when the vintage is first used. Once a production unit is brought into use no further technical change occurs. Allen shows that, if factors are paid their marginal products, an aggregate function of the form

$$Y_t = C^{gt}K_t^{\alpha}L_t^{1-\alpha} \qquad (8.2)$$

will exist so long as capital is measured in terms of equivalent new machines (a surrogate measure),

$$K_t = \int_{v=t-\tau}^{t} \mathrm{e}^{-(g/\alpha)(t-v)}K_v dv \qquad (8.3)$$

The conditions under which an aggregate function, such as equation (8.2), arises are not stressed by Allen. Fisher (1969), however, has followed up the earlier work of Leontief (1947a, 1947b) and has considered the problems of aggregation in some detail. Fisher has shown that, when the underlying production functions are Cobb–Douglas, the Leontief conditions (for the existence of an aggregate production function) are satisfied if the aggregate variables are calculated as geometric means. Fisher further argued, however, that where the aggregate output and labour variables are formed as arithmetic sums (even assuming they are both homogeneous), an aggregate capital variable will exist only if the underlying production functions exhibit constant returns to scale and capital vintages differ only through the impact of disembodied capital augmenting technical progress. These two features are assumed in the Allen model.

In general, the conditions for the existence of an aggregate production function are rarely met, and it is only rarely that the available statistics are sufficiently detailed to enable geometric means to be constructed. In this case, immense problems are associated with measuring the capital input. In addition, Fisher (1969) and Blaug (1974, pp. 15–16) point to the fact that the conditions for aggregating heterogeneous labour and output are equally stringent. The estimated macro functions that have been reported in the literature cannot be rigorously justified.

Solow, realising the difficulties of rigorously justifying his empirical work, adopted a different standpoint. He claimed that, although more disaggregate models may represent higher orders of approximation to the underlying technology, the more aggregate models are equally respectable, because they propose 'empirical laws' of an aggregate type. If such functions represent aggregate laws, then it can be argued that the only tests are those of statistical validity and intuitive plausibility. Tests of this type are compatible with Solow's (1966, pp. 1259–60) prime directive that the aggregate analysis should be treated 'as an illuminating parable, or else merely a device for handling data, to be used so long as it gives good empirical results, and to be abandoned as soon as it does not, or as soon as something better comes along'. Solow's disagreement with Joan Robinson arose mainly because he believed that she was against useful, although inexact, constructions such as the aggregate Cobb–Douglas function without providing a better substitute (see Wan, 1971, p. 97).

Solow's point is undoubtedly a good one. Economists are only too pleased to make use of 'empirical laws' when, for example, they are attempting to make forecasts. Unfortunately, however, although the function continues to perform well empirically, its intuitive plausibility has been increasingly called into question. The implausible assumptions about the capital input have led to a movement towards models based on heterogeneous capital goods. In addition, a number of economists have argued that particular features of the data cause the Cobb–Douglas phenomenon. This raises the important question of what, if anything, is being tested when an aggregate Cobb–Douglas function is estimated?

### 'As if': an inadequate defence

The neoclassicists' main defence of their empirical results has been to argue that observed points behave 'as if' they are consistent with a neoclassical technology. However, when forced to justify this proposition, they were unable to find any adequate theoretical reasons. In this section we take a look at the two principal surrogate production-function models and the Houthakker–Johansen approach.

*Surrogate production functions.* The initial stimulus to the stream of surrogate theory was provided by Joan Robinson (1953–54). It was assumed that there existed a finite number of fixed-coefficient technologies (the 'book of blueprints'). Real capital, $K_L$, was measured in labour units. Its size was determined by the number of labour units used in its construction, compounded at the relevant rate of interest over the gestation period for that type of capital, $L_K(1+i)^t$. The value of capital, on which the rate of interest ($i$) was hung, was the real capital weighted by the wage rate ($w$). Hence, in the simplest possible case, the accounting tautology for any particular technology was written

$$Y = i[wL_K(1+i)^t] + wL \qquad (8.4)$$

Given $Y$, $L_K$ and $L$ for each process, it was then possible to isolate the $r$ that corresponded to any particular $w$. By comparing all of the alternative techniques in the 'book of blueprints', the equipment that yielded the greatest profit was found.

Points on a pseudo-production function were derived by comparing the choices made from the 'book of blueprints' by a number of isolated islands characterised by different wage regimes. The resulting distribution of points in the input–output space formed a linear programming type of function, characterised by horizontal stretches at the points where the function changed slope. The pseudo-production function is represented by the unbroken line in Figure 8.1. The horizontal stretches were caused by different valuations of a given piece of capital on two different islands.

Solow (1956, p. 101) commented on this rather peculiar result, arguing that 'from the point of view of production, two identical plants represent two identical plants'. Champernowne (1953–54) also was worried about this particular feature of the pseudo-production function and, not heeding Joan Robinson's warnings, [2] proceeded to chain-link the capital values and treated the function 'as if' substitution were possible. The result was the more usual linear programming form

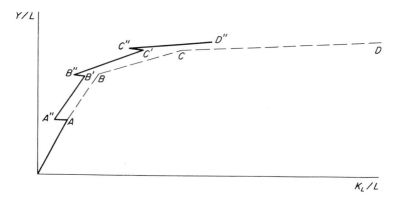

Fig. 8.1   The pseudo-production function

0$ABCD$ in Figure 8.1. Harcourt (1972, p. 32) neatly summarised the result: 'in effect Champernowne has removed the "zigs" – the horizontal stretches – from Joan Robinson's real-factor-ratio . . . and changed the slopes of the "zags" – the upward sloping stretches – so that they now equal the relevant equilibrium values of the "price" of "capital".'

As Champernowne astutely realised, chain-linking produced the desired characteristics in the manipulated function only so long as: (a) the particular technique that proved to be the most profitable at a given rate of interest (or range of rates) did not reappear at another rate (or range of rates); and (b), of two techniques that proved equally profitable at a given rate of interest, the technique with the lower capital intensity and output per head proved the more profitable at a higher rate of interest. Under these assumptions Champernowne was able to translate the production function 0$ABCD$ into a well-behaved wage–interest frontier.

Samuelson (1962) chose to work directly in the wage–interest space. In a world characterised by heterogeneous capital goods, he allowed technologies drawn from the 'book of blueprints' to be dominated by technologies that had wage–interest lines lying further to the north-east in the wage–interest space. Under a number of assumptions (the stringency of which was not immediately recognised), the wage–interest frontier was shown to be well behaved, as illustrated in Figure 8.2.

Each wage–interest line can be represented by an equation of the form

$$w = \frac{1}{\xi^L} - \frac{\xi^K}{\xi^L} i \tag{8.5}$$

where $\xi^K$ and $\xi^L$ denote input per unit of output coefficients for capital and labour respectively. Using these equations it is possible to translate directly from the wage–interest space to the input–output space, and *vice versa*, remembering only that as we move around a wage–interest frontier we move from one equation to another. Harcourt (1972, pp. 131–44) has demonstrated that the Samuelson model satisfies the four neoclassical postulates:

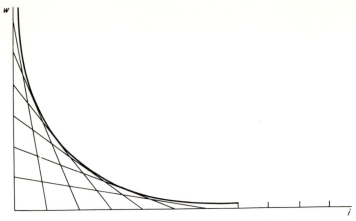

Fig. 8.2   A well-behaved wage–interest frontier

(1)   lower rates of profits are associated with higher capital per man;
(2)   lower rates of profits are associated with higher capital–output ratios;
(3)   lower rates of profits imply higher sustainable steady-states of consumption per head; and
(4)   under competitive conditions, the distribution of income between profit receivers and wage earners can be explained by a knowledge of marginal products and factor supplies.

Thus, so long as the appropriate surrogate measure of capital was used $\left(K = -L\dfrac{dw}{di}\right)$, the Samuelson approach resulted in a surrogate production function

$$Y = F(K, L) \qquad (8.6)$$

possessing the desired neoclassical properties. Had even this event passed without criticism, the fact would have remained that this result is a long way from being a justification of the aggregate production-function estimates that have appeared in the literature. To take just one aspect, the capital-stock variables used in the literature are not measured consistently with Samuelson's surrogate variable. In addition, there is no reason to suppose that the surrogate function can throw any light on the reason why the results obtained in time-series studies differ from those obtained in cross-sectional studies. In practice, the surrogate production function has been discredited on theoretical grounds. An important deficiency of it is that it is a long-run equilibrium position and no attempt has been made to analyse the way in which the economy adjusts towards this equilibrium. The most telling criticism that has appeared in the literature has concerned the assumption of wage–interest lines.

The wage–interest function becomes concave to the origin when the capital-good activity is more capital intensive than the consumption-good activity (and *vice versa* for convexity). This immediately implies the demise of the link with marginal-productivity theory. In addition, however, non-linear relationships give rise to the possibility of capital reversing and capital reswitching. These two phenomena can arise if the two assumptions made by Champernowne do not hold. In this case, the unique monotonic relationships between $w$ and $K/L$ and between $i$ and $K/L$ assumed in Samuelson's parable are no longer valid, and a surrogate production function with neoclassical properties can no longer be isolated.

Capital reversing and reswitching are generally associated with the fact that physical capital can be valued differently under different factor- or product-price regimes. Reversing and reswitching may prove to be common events in a world of heterogeneous capital goods characterised by a variety of time patterns of costs and revenues. It seems all the more surprising, therefore, that Sato (1974, pp. 354–5) should have claimed that, by the inclusion of a technology frontier in this type of model, the neoclassical postulate is 'unqualifiedly valid when certain plausible conditions are met by the technology frontier'. The Sato approach may play an important role in an integrated production system of the Johansen (1972) kind, but it does not (as Sato claims) provide an all-embracing answer to the 'Cambridge controversy'. The reason is simply that Sato (1974, p. 357) assumes that capital is measured in physical units, and this places important aspects of the reswitching and reversing phenomena 'out of bounds'. In fact, dealing in a world of instantaneous capital measured in physical units, the neoclassical postulate was never in any real danger: it is the difference in valuation of capital in different wage–interest regimes that is the underlying cause of the phenomena.

A paper by Pyatt (1963) has suggested that it is possible to move from a putty-clay world [3] to a surrogate production function of the Samuelson kind by a more direct route. Pyatt claims that the main advantage of this approach is that it does not depend on the existence of equilibrium market conditions or of any particular theory of income distribution. It does, however, rely on profit-maximising behaviour. From a vintage starting point, it works its way to a growth-accounting equation similar to the one that appeared in Solow's pioneering paper (1957):

$$\frac{\dot{Y}}{Y} = \frac{i\kappa}{pY}\left(\frac{\dot{\kappa}}{\kappa}\right) + \frac{wL}{pY}\left(\frac{\dot{L}}{L}\right) \tag{8.7}$$

where $\cdot$ denotes time derivatives and $\kappa$ is a surrogate measure of the capital input, such that

$$\frac{\dot{\kappa}}{\kappa} = \frac{p\dot{Y} - w\dot{L}}{\Pi} \tag{8.8}$$

where $\Pi$ denotes total profit. There is no doubt that the empirical results in the literature are not based on such a measure of the capital input and this approach cannot be used as an explanation of the Cobb–Douglas result. Finally, no investigation of the properties of the surrogate production function was undertaken and no evidence exists to suggest that it could provide any insights about the divergence of time-series and cross-sectional results.

*The Houthakker–Johansen approach.* An alternative approach that may provide a justification for the neoclassical production function arises from work undertaken originally by Houthakker (1955–56) and extended by Johansen (1972). The basic model assumes the existence of a large number of independent fixed-coefficient production units. Each production unit is a substitute for every other unit in the sense that it produces an identical output. The total of such units is the 'region of positive capacity', which is divided into two half-spaces by a separating plane formed by the zero quasi-rent line. The half-space comprised of the economically viable production units is called the 'utilised region'.

For any given zero quasi-rent line, the points within the region can be summed to form $Y$, $K$ and $L$ (in the two-input case) where inputs are measured in physical units. Here, in order to provide consistency with the remainder of the analysis, capital is treated as a current input. Johansen, however, finds it more meaningful to assume capital is a special, fixed factor.

The relationship $Y = F(K, L)$ is called the short-run macro function. Problems of aggregation are avoided simply by assuming that a sufficiently large number of input categories are distinguished to ensure that each is internally homogeneous (see Hahn and Matthews, 1964, p. 110). The exact magnitudes of the aggregate variables are determined by the distribution of established capacity in the utilised region. As the zero quasi-rent line swings or shifts, the utilised region changes, admitting new production units (with different technical characteristics) and evicting existing units. The result is that $Y$, $K$ and $L$ change.

Johansen (1972, pp. 52–62) has shown that, if output is held constant but the zero quasi-rent line is allowed to shift, the aggregate production isoquant

$$\xi^K = g(\xi^L) \tag{8.9}$$

is consistent with the basic neoclassical postulate. That is, as the line swings in the direction of higher wage–rental values, relatively labour-intensive units leave the utilised region and relatively capital-intensive units enter. Indeed, with full mathematical rigour, Johansen was able to show that $w$ and $r$ are the marginal products of this aggregate function:

$$\frac{\partial Y}{\partial K} = r \quad \text{and} \quad \frac{\partial Y}{\partial L} = w \tag{8.10}$$

where the slope of the isoquant is given by

$$\left.\frac{dL}{dK}\right|_{dY=0} = -\frac{r}{w} \tag{8.11}$$

As an explanation of the Cobb–Douglas empirical phenomenon, however, this type of approach has important deficiencies. First, the short-run macro function exhibits decreasing returns to scale at all levels of activity. Second, the elasticity of substitution between factors is determined by a number of features of the technology –

(1)  the variety of technologies at the margin,
(2)  the absolute level of operations,
(3)  the amount of production capacity located in a small strip close to the zero quasi-rent line –

and there is no immediately apparent reason why the elasticity of substitution should be unity. Finally, the capital input is measured in real terms and this avoids problems of revaluation as the zero quasi-rent line shifts. If capital were measured in value terms, then, as the quasi-rent line shifted, the distribution of points in the input per unit of output space could change as capital was revalued. Under these circumstances there is no reason why the isoquant should retain the desired neo-classical properties.

## The Cobb–Douglas function: an empirical accident

A number of authors have attempted to demonstrate that the Cobb–Douglas function is an empirical accident that is largely unconnected with the technology of production. Brown (1957, pp. 552–7), for example, [4] has produced evidence about a cross-section of Australian industries in 1912. He found that points in the input–output space fell within a narrow tube with a 45° slope to each co-ordinate plane. The explanation for this was that inputs and outputs had changed at much the same rate in all industries. This feature of the data was sufficient to ensure that constant returns to scale existed in the estimated function. In addition, comparison of the accounting identity

$$p_j Y_j = r_j K_j + w_j L_j \qquad (8.12)$$

with a Cobb–Douglas function of the form

$$Y_j = A K_j^\alpha L_j^{1-\alpha} \qquad (8.13)$$

revealed that the estimated coefficients $\alpha$ and $1-\alpha$ would reflect factor shares

$$\alpha = \frac{r_j K_j}{p_j Y_j} \quad \text{and} \quad 1-\alpha = \frac{w_j L_j}{p_j Y_j} \qquad (8.14)$$

as long as factor prices did not vary greatly across industries.

The explanation has been revised by Cramer (1969, pp. 236–7). He argued that, because the accounting tautology holds, any function fitted to the set of points $\{Y, K, L\}$ will tend to give a good statistical fit. More importantly, however, he argued that, when there was not a great deal of variation in the sample, the log-linear function could be manipulated into linear form:

$$Y_j = \alpha \frac{\overline{Y}}{\overline{K}} K_j + \beta \frac{\overline{Y}}{\overline{L}} L_j + (1-\alpha-\beta)\overline{Y} \qquad (8.15)$$

where $\overline{Y}, \overline{K}$ and $\overline{L}$ denote geometric sample means. Comparison with the accounting equation indicated that

129

$$\alpha \frac{\overline{Y}}{\overline{K}} \sim \frac{r}{p} \quad \text{or} \quad \alpha \sim \frac{r\overline{K}}{p\overline{Y}}$$

$$\beta \frac{\overline{Y}}{\overline{L}} \sim \frac{w}{p} \quad \text{or} \quad \beta \sim \frac{w\overline{L}}{p\overline{Y}} \tag{8.16}$$

$$(1-\alpha-\beta)\overline{Y} \sim 0 \quad \text{or} \quad \alpha+\beta \sim 1$$

where $\overline{Y} > 0$.

Sufficient variation in the data is essential if the results derived are to be meaningful. Johansen (1972, p. 184) has pointed out that the very act of stratifying data in a technically meaningful way may cut the degree of variation down to a level that is insufficient to reveal the true underlying technology. No one, it appears, has tested the degree of variation that is sufficiently small to cause the Brown–Cramer result. One suspects, however, that the degree of variation in the data used in a number of studies has been considerable and that some additional explanation is required.

Fisher (1971) attempted to isolate the reason why aggregate Cobb–Douglas functions performed well even though they could not be rigorously justified. This involved a large number of simulation experiments, fitting Cobb–Douglas functions to data that, when aggregated, were known to be inconsistent with this technology. The inappropriateness of the aggregate data was ensured by violating the conditions for the existence of an aggregate capital stock.

The estimates were based on time-series information, but the conclusions are nonetheless relevant to this study. Without exception the reported functions generated high $R^2$, but this was simply the result of the variables trending over time. Under these circumstances, an aggregate function tends to fit well whether or not it is misspecified. As $R^2$ was not particularly sensitive and because interest centred on the explanation of wages, a root-mean-square measure of the deviation of actual from predicted wages was chosen as a measure of performance.

Over 830 experiments were carried out and the key result established was that the success of the aggregate Cobb–Douglas function was the result of the relative constancy of labour's share. Fisher (1971, p. 307) noted that

> The point of our results, however, is not that an aggregate Cobb–Douglas function fails to work well when labour's share ceases to be roughly constant, it is that an aggregate Cobb–Douglas function will continue to work well so long as labour's share continues to be roughly constant, even though that rough constancy is not itself a consequence of the economy having a technology that is truly summarised by an aggregate Cobb–Douglas.

Fisher provides a useful piece of information: that we may expect a Cobb–Douglas function to arise when factor shares are roughly constant, whether or not the technology of production in the economy is Cobb–Douglas. We are left wondering, however, what part is played by the underlying neoclassical technologies. Would the results have been consistent with an aggregate Cobb–Douglas function if the micro technologies had been fixed-coefficient? It seems likely, for example, that the further we move away from neoclassical micro technologies, the less certain it is that constant factor shares are sufficient to ensure the good empirical performance of the aggregate relationship.

## The surrogate production function: an alternative view

An attempt is made here to combine some of the more revealing parts of the existing explanations of the good empirical performance of the Cobb–Douglas function. The principal aim is to explain why cross-sectional observations are often consistent with a Cobb–Douglas function exhibiting constant returns to scale. The argument put forward here is that this result arises because of the way in which the inputs have been measured in most empirical studies. It is argued that the peculiar use of the value of capital to represent the capital input – called by Joan Robinson (1970) the 'strangest part of the whole affair' – provides a valuable clue to a viable explanation of the neoclassical result.

The starting point is the accounting tautology, which forms the basis of Cramer's explanation of the Cobb–Douglas result (see Cramer, 1969). Only aggregate inputs, $K$ and $L$, are distinguished, because it is believed that it is on the basis of accounting information of this kind that firms make their more important decisions. An accounting relationship is assumed to exist for each firm in a particular industry, which is made up from a large number of firms producing identical outputs sold in a single product market. The output of the industry is produced by firms in a number of different regions experiencing different factor prices. These assumptions are combined with two further theories about firm behaviour: first, that firms attempt to relocate themselves in order to produce at lowest cost per unit of output; and, second, that, where relocation does not reduce unit costs sufficiently for firms to remain competitive, the firms in question can undertake defensive innovation.

We adopt a surrogate approach directly in the input–output space rather than in the factor-price space (as in the case of Samuelson's 1962 work). The surrogate arises at the accounting–technology interface under the assumptions made above. In this way we derive a long-run frontier function with neoclassical characteristics. These conditions are, however, consistent with a wide variety of functions, only one of which will be the Cobb–Douglas function.

In order to derive a Cobb–Douglas function from the neoclassical alternatives, it is necessary to make a further assumption. Fisher's 1971 study indicated that a set of institutional forces that keep factor shares reasonably constant could give rise to the good empirical performance of the Cobb–Douglas function. In the context of this study, the assumption of constant factor shares is sufficient to collapse the wide variety of production functions to the Cobb–Douglas formulation. Whether this assumption is justifiable is a matter for empirical verification. Allen (1968) and Fisher (1969) have shown that it is a simple matter to aggregate using arithmetic sums only if the underlying neoclassical functions are Cobb–Douglas with constant returns to scale, where capital inputs differ only through the impact of disembodied technical changes. These conditions can now be shown to be satisfied, allowing aggregation over industries even given the way particular inputs are aggregated in official statistics.

*The accounting identity*

Cramer (1969) suggested that we should look more closely at the accounting identity:

$$p_j Y_j = i_j K_j + w_j L_j \qquad (8.17)$$

where $K$ is an accounting measure of the capital stock. His reason was that not only would a large number of functions involving $Y$, $K$ and $L$ tend to fit the data well, but, in addition, a lack of variation in the data would cause the coefficients from a log-linear formulation (such as the Cobb–Douglas function) to be equal to factor shares. There is no evidence regarding what degree of variation is required to break this link: but here, for the sake of argument, it is assumed that a great deal of variation does exist.

A number of important assumptions are made. First, all firms belong to the same industry and sell their final produce in a single, highly competitive market. Second, for one reason or another, firms experience a wide variety of wage–interest values. One cause of such diversity may be the existence of production units in a number of different geographical regions. Finally, it is also assumed that factor markets are highly competitive. In the case of regional factor markets, we are simply implying that within each market there exist a large number of buyers (production units) and sellers of factor services, forcing abnormal profits down to zero in long-run equilibrium.

On the basis of these assumptions, we can rewrite equation (8.17) omitting the subscript $j$ on price. Hence

$$p = i_j \frac{K_j}{Y_j} + w_j \frac{L_j}{Y_j} = i_j \xi_j^K + w_j \xi_j^L \qquad (8.18)$$

If we draw the price line associated with a given firm, $F_A$, in the input per unit of output space, it will appear as $P_A$ in Figure 8.3. The price line is denoted by $P$, and a point drawn from that line is denoted by $p$. Firm $F_A$ chooses to produce at point $A$ on the price line $P_A$ defined by $p = i_A \xi_A^K + w_A \xi_A^L$. All the points in the rectangular quadrant to the north-east of $A$ are revealed to be less preferred than point $A$. All such points can be attained without having to introduce real technical changes, because they can be reached simply by hoarding more of one or both inputs. Given the factor costs that $F_A$ faces, all such points would involve higher costs of production per unit of output and would be inconsistent with the accounting identity. We know nothing about any of the points lying between the quadrant with corner point $A$ and the horizontal and vertical axes. All we can say is that the set of such points is technically different from the set in the quadrant with corner point $A$, and that a subset of them will be technically superior.

There is nothing to prevent the existence of a plant that has lower technical efficiency (i.e. uses more of both inputs per unit of output) but produces in a region

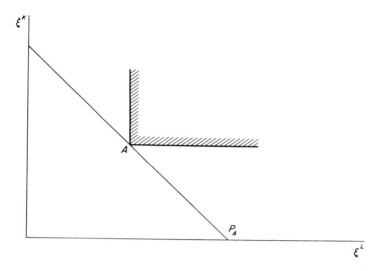

Fig. 8.3   Plant equilibrium in the input per unit output space

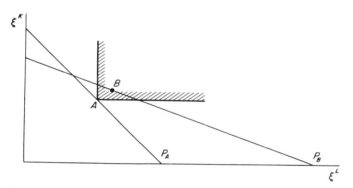

Fig. 8.4   Existence of technically inferior production units

with lower factor costs. Such a firm could still satisfy the accounting identity. Figure 8.4 illustrates this case where $p_A = p_B = p$. In this way it is possible for all points in the input per unit of output space to be feasible.

*Domination and the long-run equilibrium position*

We now impose the condition that, if an existing technology of production would lower the costs of production for a given firm, then in the long run it will be adopted by the firm. Alternatively, if a firm with a particular technology of production could lower its unit costs by moving to a new region, then in the long run it will relocate its productive activity. In the case of $F_A$ and $F_B$ the adjustment is as shown in Figure 8.5.

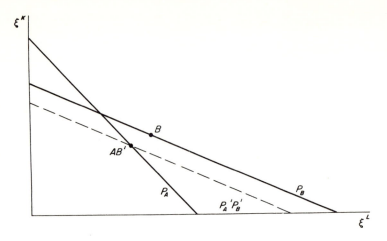

Fig. 8.5   Towards the long-run equilibrium function

When $F_B$ adopts the technology of $F_A$ (or alternatively, $F_A$ moves its more efficient technology to a region of lower resource costs) the price per unit of output falls from $p$ to $p'$, where $p > p'$.

The nature of the equilibrium situation is fairly easy to see. At a given wage–interest ratio there can exist only one price line that corresponds to the combination of the lowest resource costs with the most efficient technology. Where lines of different slopes have points that lie inside other price lines, as indeed point $A$ dominated point $B$ above, further inward shifts in the price lines will occur. Only when all remaining points lie on a single boundary line, analogous to Samuelson's frontier, will all the forces for change disappear. If there exists a sufficiently wide variety of alternative wage–interest ratios, then the frontier takes on the shape of a well behaved neoclassical isoquant similar to that shown in Figure 8.2 but with axes $\xi^K$ and $\xi^L$.

This function is consistent with neoclassical theory. If we can assume that in the long run such a function evolves, then a single, 'well-behaved' function in the input per unit of output space has been derived. A direct implication is that we can transform the function from its present form,

$$\xi^K = g(\xi^L) \tag{8.19}$$

into a production function,

$$Y = f(K, L) \tag{8.20}$$

*Returns to scale in the surrogate production function*

What returns to scale are consistent with the surrogate relationship? The model ensures, via its assumption of perfectly competitive factor markets within each region, that factor prices are the same for all production units in a particular region.

134

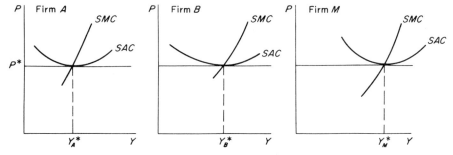

Fig. 8.6  Firm equilibrium positions

The nature of the long-run solution ensures that there will be, at most, only one efficient technology (defined in terms of overall inputs per unit of output – $\xi^K$, $\xi^L$) for each region, which is consistent with the price condition.

Each firm can have a different cost curve in a world where firms are characterised by different heterogeneous sets of capital and labour. The model, however, imposes one common characteristic on the set of possible cost curves. All firms that are to continue in existence in the long run (i.e. are to be represented by a point on the surrogate function) must produce at the minimum point on their average-cost curve, and all such minimum points must be at a common price, $p^*$.

The model can be demonstrated to be consistent with U-shaped firm cost curves. The firm equilibrium positions are shown in Figure 8.6 and market equilibrium in Figure 8.7.

The nature of the long-run equilibrium position dictates that no firm possesses

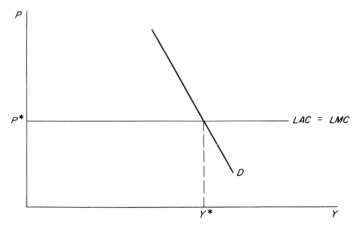

Fig. 8.7  Industry equilibrium

the technology and management expertise necessary to enter at a lower price per unit of output than $p^*$, and firms attempting to establish production units at a higher price are automatically eliminated by the forces of competition. Hence, the minimum points of the short-run average-cost curves, which are all at one common price, define the long-run average-cost curve, which is the envelope of all such cost curves and can be represented as a horizontal line, as in Figure 8.7. The intersection with the demand curve determines the industry output $Y^*$. Each firm in the industry is in long-run equilibrium as each firm is equating its marginal cost with its marginal revenue. In long-run equilibrium, each firm is at the point on its cost curve consistent with constant returns to scale.

The model is obviously inconsistent with firms whose cost curves exhibit increasing returns to scale at all levels of output. This would imply that any particular firm could always lower its price by raising its level of production. Taken to its logical conclusion, this implies that a single firm would eventually take over, and cater for the whole of market demand. The set of possible price lines consistent with the surrogate function collapses to a single line. Increasing returns to scale over all levels of output is obviously inconsistent with perfect competition in both the product and the factor markets.

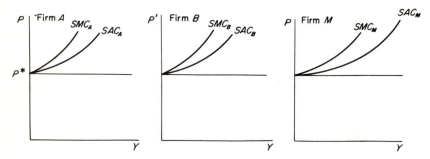

Fig. 8.8    Firm equilibrium under decreasing returns to scale

The case where firms in the industry all experience decreasing returns to scale over the whole range of possible outputs is more bizarre. The degree of peculiarity depends mainly on whether there is a positive minimum scale of operation for the firm. Figure 8.8 demonstrates what happens when the cost curves emanate from a point on the vertical (price) axis. The industry supply curve (which is again the envelope of all the firm's supply curves) and industry equilibrium can still be represented by Figure 8.7.

The long-run cost curve is formed as the envelope of all the minimum points on the cost curves of individual firms. But, at this price level, firms in the industry produce no output. This is a particular case that is inconsistent with long-run equilibrium. In the case where there is a minimum size of firm (perhaps dictated by technical conditions) this peculiar market situation collapses to the more normal, U-shaped solution. The number of firms is now dictated by the minimum size of output that firms are willing to produce. The long-run cost curves can, in both cases, be treated as horizontal, and returns to scale are constant.

The result of constant returns to scale is an important one. The existence of this feature is crucial to the ease of aggregation over industries. It cannot be emphasised too strongly, however, that its existence in this model depends on the assumptions that have been made about market structure.

*The adjustment process*

Samuelson (1962) was content to establish the nature of a possible long-run equilibrium situation without describing the adjustment process that would enable it to be attained. The adjustment process is more important in the present study, because an explanation of the good empirical performance of the Cobb–Douglas function will depend on the adjustment resulting in points on a number of price lines. There is no reason, however, why the adjustment process, as we have specified it so far (relying solely on domination arising from combining efficient technologies with the cheapest factor supplies), should result in more than one price line, except by chance.

The introduction of technical change alongside the efficient use of existing resources may provide one solution to the problem. If we consider $F_A$ and $F_B$ again, we might assume that $F_A$ has the more efficient technology and the higher quality of management. If $F_B$ is unable to learn of and adopt the more efficient technology, it

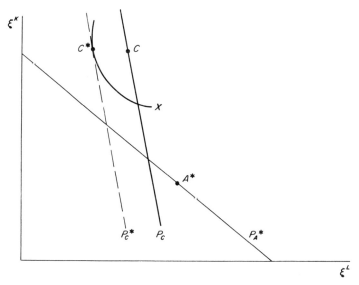

Fig. 8.9   Long-run equilibrium with technical change

will go out of business. Let us assume that $F_C$ can dominate its rivals in a similar way to $F_A$. If the resulting price lines are $P_C$ and $P_A^*$, where $p_C > p_A^*$, then, if further technical changes are not possible, $F_C$ will be dominated by $F_A$ and disappear. If, however, $F_C$ can gain the technical knowledge necessary to shift its price line inwards, and then innovate appropriately, it may yet survive. The manner in which the technical change is made is assumed to depend on the nature of $F_C$'s T-isocost map $X$. (See Nordhaus, 1974.) If each member of the T-isocost map is well behaved, equilibrium (based on the cost-minimising level of R & D and innovative expenditure) will be at point $C^*$ in Figure 8.9, where $p_C^* = p_A^*$.

### A more general accounting identity

In principle there is no reason why we cannot insert a more realistic accounting identity. Abnormal short-run profits are introduced, a transitory feature, and are bid away in the long run. The price line for the $j$th firm can now be written:

$$p_j Y_j = i_j K_j + w_j L_j + \Pi_j \qquad (8.21)$$

or

$$p = i_j \xi_j^K + w_j \xi_j^L + \pi_j \qquad (8.22)$$

where, $\pi_j (= \Pi_j / Y_j)$ is profit per unit of output. Rather than set transitory profits equal to zero in the long run, a normal rate of profit per unit of output can be introduced directly into the function, $\pi^*$. Firms will now remain in the industry in the long run only if $\pi_j \geqq \pi^*$, but competitive forces ensure that $\pi_j = \pi^*$. In this case, the long-run frontier function is simply a shifted version of its former self.

In the short run, profits add a degree of flexibility that was not there previously. For example,

(a) $\Pi > \Pi^*$ may provide an incentive for new firms to enter and for existing firms (earning less profit, i.e. $\Pi < \Pi^*$) to review their current technology and location; (b) when a firm is losing out to a technically more efficient and/or better located competitor, a reduction in its profits such that $\Pi < \Pi^*$ may enable the firm to remain in business, while $\Pi > 0$ implies that the firm can finance defensive R & D and innovation.

### Constant factor shares and the Cobb–Douglas function

What we have argued is that, within a particular industry, there may exist forces that move aggregate (i.e. firm-level) fixed-coefficient technologies ($\xi^K$, $\xi^L$) towards a 'well-behaved' isoquant with constant returns to scale. We have, though, not yet succeeded in isolating a Cobb–Douglas function, because a wide variety of functions are consistent with this result. If, however, we add the assumption of institutionally determined constant relative factor shares to our 'well-behaved' function, this is sufficient to produce a Cobb–Douglas function. The realism of the assumption again turns on its empirical validity.

If the model described above is correct, then a Cobb–Douglas function with constant returns to scale describes each industry. So long as this is true at some level of aggregation (no matter how detailed), the work of Fisher (1969) indicates that aggregation across industries will generally be possible and an aggregate Cobb–Douglas function will result.

## The derived function and the underlying technology of production

The movement towards a unique frontier function is associated with the profit-maximising behaviour of the firm. The long-run survival of the firm is ensured only by active policies of relocation and defensive R & D and innovation. Firms work on both their factor costs and their technical efficiency in order to ensure their continued existence.

One thing is certain, however: the frontier function is not a purely technical relationship determined independently of factor prices. It cannot, for example, be compared with the *ex ante* function. The unit of observation is assumed to be the firm and, although the frontier function represents an efficient long-run equilibrium situation, each point on the function represents a particular mix of capital types, vintages and stages of depreciation. It is in a sense a 'best practice' function, but one intimately connected with factor costs.

We have said very little about the underlying technology of production. The micro technologies can now be fixed-coefficient. The only constraint on them is that the stocks of inputs used in production should, when aggregated according to accounting principles, sum to the values that appear in the accounting identity. It is the firm accounts that form the interface between the commercial and technical characteristics of the firm.

## Conclusions

The above review of the literature indicates that the existing theories do not give an adequate explanation of why the Cobb–Douglas function performs well empirically. Aspects of a number of the more important theories were adopted in an attempt to provide a more realistic explanation. It was argued that strategic decisions made by management would be based on aggregate accounting information. This information is in the form of key variables that appear also in traditional work on production functions. The theory developed is based on the assumption that management attempts to maximise profits in the long run, on the basis of information that appears in the accounting identity. The existence of a Cobb–Douglas function is shown where there is a large degree of variation in the variables. Where this is not the case, the Brown–Cramer result can be expected.

In order to survive in the long run, the firm attempts to reduce factor prices to the lowest level possible, even if this implies the relocation of production facilities. In addition, particularly when profits fall below some desired level, the firm is assumed to search for greater technical efficiency in its use of factors of production, by adopting existing and developing new techniques. The theory suggests that in periods of prosperity ($\pi > \pi^*$) firms tend to relax their search for greater efficiency, and managerial slack appears. In periods of recession ($\pi < \pi^*$) a stimulus appears to lower costs and raise profit levels, resulting in movement towards the long-run equilibrium function. In addition, during periods of economic hardship, the least efficient production units (which are those furthest from the 'best-practice' boundary) will tend to disappear from the system. As economic activity turns upwards, units of the latest vintage (the technologies of which are close to the frontier) will begin to appear in regions of the lowest factor prices. These factors will tend to move the distribution of points towards the 'best-practice' frontier.

The model adopted is broadly in line with Williamson's (1970) view of $M$-form organisations: subgoals may be followed in the short run and at low levels in the managerial hierarchy, but the overriding long-run consideration is profitability. In the model developed here, top management is assumed to be profit maximising (on the basis of inadequate accounting information), while production managers 'satisfice' by reducing input per unit of output to acceptable levels (defined by the profit performance of the firm). There is some indication in the work of Piore (1968) and Bell (1972) that the aggregate basis on which decisions are formulated percolates through to induced technical change. Their studies indicate that broad market trends (rather than those associated with particular input categories) affect the pattern of technical change.

The 'best-practice' boundary is a surrogate production function with neoclassical properties. 'Best-practice' in this sense implies a very practical efficient boundary (unlike the Johansen long-run macro function, where all capital is moulded into the very latest vintage) where it is recognised to be efficient to hold capital of different types and ages. Constant factor shares at the micro level is sufficient to collapse the neoclassical class of functions to a Cobb–Douglas function. The existence of micro Cobb–Douglas functions exhibiting constant returns to scale and with capital measured in common (value) units is sufficient to ensure that the aggregate functions have the same form. In this way, the theory developed in this paper gives some explanation of the aggregate relationship that economists often estimate. To call this a production function, however, is extremely misleading. The stocks of physical inputs that constitute the aggregate variables may differ from firm to firm and every firm can be considered as an amalgamation of different types and ages of capital and labour. These physical aspects of production are largely obscured by the value measure adopted in the relationship. The resulting Cobb–Douglas function is consistent with a wide variety of underlying engineering functions.

## Notes

[1] For the reader who is not convinced of the case against the existence of aggregate neoclassical production functions, see Blaug (1974, chapter 2).

[2] For example, Joan Robinson (1970, pp. 103–4) warned that, 'To move from

one point to another we would have either to rewrite past history or to embark upon a long future.'

[3] In a later paper, Pyatt (1964a) has demonstrated that the same result can be shown for a putty–putty vintage world.

[4] A similar explanation is provided in a paper by Heathfield (1972b).

# 9 Production functions – some conclusions

Existing theoretical and empirical research has focused on determining the realism of the vintage and neoclassical approaches as a crucial step in the development of a realistic theory of production. It is even more important, however, to delimit the situations where a production function is an appropriate basis for empirical research. Economists have looked no further than the theory of production to explain macro relationships, although it is fairly obvious that other factors are at work. While technical relationships can be expected to dominate the micro scene, aspects of market structure and industrial performance can be expected to become increasingly important at higher levels of aggregation.

A cross-sectional approach has been adopted in this study. This is generally thought to be most applicable where long-run equilibrium situations are being considered. Estimation has been undertaken for a number of consecutive years, and this has made it possible to obtain a time series of estimated coefficients. Repeated estimation of this kind allows the stability of the estimated coefficients over time to be observed. In addition, if a sufficiently long time series of coefficients can be obtained, there is the possibility of finding explanatory variables for them. This may enable future values of coefficients to be predicted and may provide the starting point for constructing simultaneous systems. It is an important criticism of most of the time-series work on production and employment functions that models are not re-estimated for subperiods in order to test the stability of the parameters, and that, in making predictions, the estimated coefficients are assumed to remain constant over quite long periods. The empirical exercise undertaken in this book can be viewed as a prelude to a more rigorous forecasting exercise where, given confidence intervals for the predicted coefficients, a range of predictions can be made avoiding the criticisms levelled at single-valued forecasts.

Data used in this study were drawn from the UK engineering industry. Engineering is a key sector of the economy and is a focal point for any comprehensive economic planning exercise. Planners at the national and at the industry level, aiming to assist market mechanisms to equilibrate supplies and demands of both products and factors, must eventually tread the tortuous paths of the production-function literature. Before bodies such as the Engineering Industry Training Board can place any reliance on forecasts when formulating their plans, there must be a greater understanding of the underlying relationships and a more objective view of the ability of the various models to describe and predict.

Undoubtedly a major obstacle in the path of theoretical and empirical improvements is the lack of appropriate data. Although probably more data are available for this than for any other sector, it is by no means adequate. The problem is more acute at the micro level, but it exists also at higher levels of aggregation. The nature and prevalence of shiftworking in the UK is largely undocumented. It is one case where the availability of data has deteriorated over time – the more frequent observations that have become available in the 1970s are not so detailed as their less frequent predecessors were. Utilisation is another key variable about which little or nothing is known. The CBI's quarterly survey *Industrial Trends* can provide some insights; and, while the form taken by the questions posed in the survey is not ideal, these questions have remained unchanged for a long period and the industry detail associated with them has increased considerably with the passage of time. More detailed fuel-consumption data (for the construction of 'Wharton School' indices) and information about the installed rated wattage of plant and machinery (to enable Heathfield [1] type measures to be constructed) may prove even more useful. However, other improvements will be needed before a theoretically rigorous utilisation variable can be derived from available sources of data.

The vintage models are the most affected by data constraints. The models tested in Chapters 5 and 6 were recognised to be simplistic. Certain modifications that intuition suggests would make the models more realistic (i.e. managerial behaviour not consistent with profit maximisation; *ex ante* functions other than those with classical properties; and different rates of disembodied change for different vintages) are extremely difficult to test empirically because of the wholly inadequate data.

In the light of these data problems, the results detailed in Chapters 5 and 6 are surprisingly good. Those presented in Chapter 5 are perhaps of greatest interest to the theorist. A labour-demand function of vintage form performed best of all the alternatives tested, but because of intense multicollinearity between capital of different ages, it was not possible to establish the nature and rate of embodied technical change. The *ad hoc* relationship where the average age of capital appeared suggested that the relationship was characterised by Hicks neutral technical change. Perhaps the most important conclusion was that the underlying *ex ante* function appeared to have an elasticity less than unity, probably somewhere in the region of 0·3 to 0·5. The overall strength of the primary link between a particular labour skill and the type of capital with which it is usually associated suggested that further research along these lines would prove profitable, even if the approach gave no insights about the secondary effects (i.e. on other labour skills). Training boards are often more concerned about particular skills than about overall numbers, and establishing primary relationships of these types may prove valuable. Accurate short-run forecasts of labour requirements might be made using the established links with the available investment-intentions data (i.e. from *Business Monitor*). It is an admitted criticism of this approach that none of the adjustment mechanisms (which Senker et al. were worried about in their 1975 study) has yet been investigated. In addition, the forecasts, if based on investment-intentions data, would be extremely short-run and therefore of little use in formulating any major training strategies (where up to five years may be required).

In this respect, the analysis reported in Chapter 6 may prove more appropriate.

A great deal of work has been undertaken by economists on investment functions. The existing body of theory might be drawn on to make short- to medium-term forecasts of investment levels. Alternatively, the National Economic Development Office might be able to provide information about possible future rates of investment activity. However, positive and normative exercises based on this approach are unlikely to prove satisfactory until the census defines its variables in terms that the economist, rather than the accountant, will find useful (i.e. gross investment, net investment and scrapping). There is a further need for data about second-hand transactions (i.e. purchases of second-hand machines as well as disposals).

The theoretical and empirical chapters emphasise that certain aspects of the vintage model require attention. First, the *ex ante* function, in particular, needs considerable modification and improvement if it is to play the central role that vintage theory accords it. Second, there is the important question of the role played by *ex post* modifications to vintages. If this can be shown to be an empirically important phenomenon, it may mean the demise of the simple vintage theory as we now know it and require the researcher to review the entire history of each individual machine. Third, little or nothing is known about the costs of laying up and reintroducing machines. Fourth, it is important (as noted above) to establish the amount of trading in older vintages of equipment, which may severely complicate the *ex ante* relationship.

While the Johansen study (1972) was quick to emphasise that capital–labour substitution is possible even in a world characterised by fixed-coefficient micro technologies, there are other ways in which substitution can take place. A given machine and crew may be able to undertake diverse tasks. Here the roles of changes in tooling and of machine modifications appear to be extremely important areas in need of further study. In addition, there are changes in product design – perhaps in the way in which the product is put together (i.e. cast and machined rather than machined and welded). Finally, at a more aggregate level, there are changes in product mix.

The lack of detailed information is not a valid excuse for simply estimating CES functions, or input–output models, to the exclusion of developing vintage theory and empirical work. Yet there is undoubtedly something in the argument (see Barna, 1964, p. 125) that we can gain some insights from estimating more simplistic models. Aggregate input–output tables, for example, have revealed a great deal about the structure of the economy and about the links with other economies. In a similar way, CES functions have given some insights into links between firms. There is a great danger, however, of falling into the trap of believing these to be descriptions of the underlying technology – they mask diffuse micro production relationships.

If these relationships are not descriptions of the technology but are aggregate empirical laws, it is essential to explain why they exist. This is particularly relevant in the case of the Cobb–Douglas function. While the discussion in Chapter 7 emphasises that the fit of the function has not always been as good as the reported results (i.e. $\bar{R}^2$ and $F$) have implied, there can be no doubt that the function has often performed well. One possible explanation was developed in Chapter 8. Market forces may constrain the set of technologies (defined in terms of overall input–output coefficients) that can survive for any given set of product and factor prices to appear 'as if' they are drawn from a neoclassical world. However, any particular aggregate input–output coefficients ($\xi^K$, $\xi^L$), may be associated with numerous micro technologies.

An explanation of the aggregate 'empirical law' is forced to draw on theories of firm behaviour and market structure as well as on an underlying theory of the technology of production. It would seem sensible to suggest that the theory of firm behaviour should be one that allows managerial behaviour to modify according to economic conditions, thereby varying between 'satisficing' and profit maximising. The firms that survive in the long run are those best adapted to the economic conditions. Some evidence was given at the end of Chapter 7 in support of this hypothesis (for instance, the industries with a high percentage of sales contributed by foreign-controlled enterprises, which qualitative evidence has suggested to be more competitive, were found to be technically more efficient). Thus, the approach points to a 'survival of the fittest' theory. Firms that are technically inefficient or whose technologies are inappropriate in the light of economic conditions are forced to make changes under their own management, to make adjustments under a new management, or to disappear from the production system entirely.

One further conclusion can be drawn from the rather inept performance of the CES class of functions reported here, and from the relatively more impressive performance of the 'quality' variables. Not only must the new theory provide links between the theories of technology, the firm and market structure, but also they must be more dynamic. A major criticism of the work undertaken here is that too much attention has been paid to the long-run equilibrium outcome and too little to the means by which it is reached. In terms of the empirical testing of adjustment mechanisms, it may be rewarding to pool the whole body of data (as Nerlove's 1966 study suggests).

The basic conclusions of this study are that if economists are to study production functions they must look at the micro level (more in line with the so-called 'engineering functions'), [2] and to do this they will need much more detailed and accurate data. In addition, if the aggregate CES function is not a reflection of the underlying technology, it is not possible to continue according it a central place when teaching students about production theory. The function may continue to prove useful to forecasting exercises in so far as it comes as close as any to being an aggregate 'empirical law', but it may eventually prove to be an even better tool if a viable explanation for it can be found.

## Notes

[1] See Heathfield (1972a).
[2] See, for example, Chenery (1949, 1953).

# Appendix 1   Investment by type and industry within engineering

At a number of points in the present study, investment data by type of capital good and MLH are required. Data are available in this form from 1970 onwards, published in the annual *Census of Production*. For earlier years, only the quinquennial censuses give MLH detail, while the annual sample censuses distinguish a maximum of seven industry groups. The construction of MLH investment data was based on both of these sources and the resulting information relates to the years 1958–72. It is more difficult to reconcile the post-1958 industrial classifications with those used in earlier years. It is worth adding that the annual and full censuses are collected using different sampling bases (the annual census uses the company as its sampling unit, while the full census uses the establishment), and this gives rise to a number of inconsistencies.

The estimates of investment were based on the full census totals, which were known for six of the fifteen years: 1958, 1963, 1968, and 1970–72 inclusive. Information about investment by type was obtained from the full census for each of the industry groups that appear in the sample census. For each of the years for which both full and sample census information were available, the ratios of full to sample values were constructed. The ratios for intermediate years were interpolated and all of the sample census series were adjusted by the appropriate set of ratios. The resulting values are estimates of investment by type for the seven industry groups, consistent with the full census totals.

MLH detail was obtained by calculating the MLH proportions for each of the seven industry groups in the full census years and linearly interpolating these values for intermediate years. The MLH proportions were then multiplied by the estimated investment totals for the seven industries to provide MLH estimates consistent with the full census totals.

The method was applied separately to data on acquisitions and disposals of plant and machinery, vehicles and buildings. In the case of buildings, separate purchase and sale information became available only towards the end of the period, and so the method was also applied directly to total net investment.

# Appendix 2 Fuel consumption by type of fuel and industry within engineering

The method used to construct fuel data by MLH is similar to that used for investment. In this case, information is available about fuel consumption by the UK engineering industry as a whole, annually from 1958. At this level of aggregation, detailed fuel types (coal, coke, coke oven, town and natural gas, electricity, petroleum, and creosote and pitch mixes) are separately distinguished. For most fuel categories, greater industry detail (usually for about seven industry groups within engineering) is available for the years 1961 onwards, but not always on a consumption basis and generally not giving a consistent regional coverage. The industry totals for each type of fuel were therefore made to sum to the UK total for engineering.

For each industry and type of fuel, the census information for 1958, 1963 and 1968 was used to construct MLH proportions. These were then interpolated and extrapolated to cover intermediate and later years. These ratios were then multiplied by the corresponding industry totals to provide estimates of fuel consumption by MLH, consistent with the totals for the UK engineering industry. The data for each type of fuel were then translated from original into thermal units.

# Bibliography

*Abridgements of Specifications*, Patent Office, London.

Ahamad, B. and Blaug, M., *The Practice of Manpower Forecasting*, Elsevier, Amsterdam 1973.

Allen, R. G. D., *Macro Economic Theory*, Macmillan, London 1968.

Allen, R. G. D., *Mathematical Analysis for Economists*, Macmillan, London 1969.

*Annual Report of the Comptroller General of Patents Designs and Trademarks*, HMSO.

*Annual Statement of the Overseas Trade of the UK*, Department of Trade and Industry.

Armstrong, A., *Structural Change in the British Economy: 1948–1968*, in the series 'A Programme for Growth', Chapman and Hall, London 1974.

Arrow, K. J., Chenery, H. B., Minhas, B. S. and Solow, R. M., 'Capital Labour Substitution and Economic Efficiency', *Review of Economics and Statistics*, 1961.

Bacon, R. W. and Eltis, W. A., *The Age of US and UK Machinery*, National Economic Development Office, 1974.

Ball, R. J. and St Cyr, E. B. A., 'Short Term Employment Functions in British Manufacturing Industry', *Review of Economic Studies*, 1966.

Barna, T., 'A Production Functional Model – A comment', in P. E. Hart et al. (eds), *Econometric Analysis for Economic Planning*, Butterworth, London 1964.

Baumol, W. J., *Business Behaviour, Value and Growth*, Harcourt, Brace and World, New York 1959.

Baumol, W. J., 'Models of economic competition', in P. Langhoff (ed.), *Models, Measurement and Marketing*, Prentice Hall, 1965.

Baumol, W. J. and Quandt, R. E., 'Dual Prices and Competition' in R. A. Oxenfelt (ed.), *Models of Markets*, Columbia University Press 1963.

Bell, R. M., *Changing Technology and Manpower Requirements*, Sussex University Press in conjunction with the Engineering Industry Training Board 1972.

Blaug, M., 'Approaches to Educational Planning', *Economic Journal*, 1967.

Blaug, M., *An Introduction to the Economics of Education*, Allen and Unwin, London 1970.

Blaug, M., *The Cambridge Revolution: Success or Failure?*, Institute of Economic Affairs, 1974.

*Blue Book*, National Income and Accounts, Government Statistical Service.

Bosworth, D. L., 'The Skill Structure of the Engineering Industry: A Demand Approach', in J. S. Wabe et al., *Manpower Forecasting for the Engineering Industry*, Occasional Paper No. 4, Engineering Industry Training Board 1974.

Bosworth, D. L., 'Production Functions and Skill Requirements', in J. S. Wabe (ed.), *Problems in Manpower Forecasting*, Saxon House, Farnborough, 1974b.

148

Bosworth, D. L., *The Technology of Production and Manpower Planning*, Occasional Paper No. 4, Department of Economics, University of Loughborough, 1975.

Bosworth, D. L., 'Hedonic Indices for Metal Working Machine Tools', *Applied Economics*, 1976 (forthcoming).

Bosworth, D. L. and Evans, G. J., 'Manpower Forecasting Techniques: A User's Guide', *Personnel Review*, 1973.

Brown, E. H. P., 'The Meaning of the Fitted Cobb–Douglas Function', *Quarterly Journal of Economics*, 1957.

Brown, M., *On the Theory and Measurement of Technological Change*, Cambridge University Press, 1966.

*Business Monitor*, Board of Trade and Industry.

*Census of Metal Working Machine Tools*, Machinery and Production Engineering.

*Census of Population*, Department of Trade and Industry.

*Census of Production*, Office of Population censuses and surveys.

Chadwick, E. S. M., 'Manpower Planning in the British Petroleum Industry', in N. A. B. Wilson, *Manpower Research*, English Universities Press 1969.

Champernowne, D. G., 'The Production Function and the Theory of Capital', *Review of Economic Studies*, 1953–54.

Chenery, H. B., 'Engineering Production Functions', *Quarterly Journal of Economics*, 1949.

Chenery, H. B., 'Process and Production Functions from Engineering Data', in W. W. Leontief et al., *Studies in the Structure of the American Economy*, Oxford University Press, New York, 1953.

Cobb, C. W. and Douglas, P. H., 'A Theory of Production', *American Economic Review Papers and Proceedings*, 1928.

Cohen, K. J. and Cyert, R. M., *The Theory of the Firm*, Prentice Hall, Englewood Cliffs, NJ 1965.

Conlisk, J., 'A Neoclassical Growth Model with Endogenously Positioned Technical Change Frontier', *Economic Journal*, 1973.

Craine, R , 'On the Service Flow from Labour', *Review of Economic Studies*, 1972.

Cramer, J. S., *Empirical Econometrics*, North Holland, Amsterdam 1969.

Cyert, R. M. and March, J. G., *A Behavioral Theory of the Firm*, Prentice Hall, Englewood Cliffs, NJ 1963.

Douglas, P. H., 'Are these Laws of Production?', *American Economic Review* 1948.

Dudley, N. A., Jenney, B. W., Bahiri, S. and Norman, R. C., *Comparative Productivity Analysis*, Report to the DEA, Department of Production, University of Birmingham, 1968.

Evans, G. J., 'The Labour Market Mechanism and the Hoarding of Manpower', in J. S. Wabe (ed.), *Problems in Manpower Forecasting*, Saxon House, Farnborough, Hants., 1974.

Fair, R. C., 'Capital – Labor Substitution and the Demand for Capacity', Discussion Paper, Princeton University, 1971.

Fellner, I., 'Production Isoquants and the Analysis of Technological and Technical Change', *Quarterly Journal of Economics*, 1973.

149

Feldstein, M. S., 'Specification of the Labour Input and the Aggregate Production Function', *Review of Economic Studies*, 1967.

Fisher, F. M., 'The Existence of Aggregate Production Functions', *Econometrica*, 1969.

Fisher, F. M., 'Aggregate Production Functions and the Explanation of Wages: A Simulation Experiment', *Review of Economics and Statistics*, 1971.

Foss, M., 'The Utilisation of Capital Equipment', *Survey of Current Business*, 43, No. 4, 1963.

Furubotn, E. G., 'Engineering Data and the Production Function', *American Economic Review*, 1965.

Ghosh, A., 'A Note on Leontief Models with Non-homogeneous Production Functions', *Metroeconomica*, 1960.

Gregory, R. G. and James, D. W., 'Do New Factories Embody Best Practice Technology?' *Economic Journal*, 1974.

Gregory, R. G. and James, D. W., 'Do New Factories Embody Best Practice Technology?: A Reply', *Economic Journal*, 1975.

Griliches, Z. and Ringstad, V., *Economics of Scale and the Form of the Production Function*, North Holland, Amsterdam 1971.

Hahn, F. H. and Matthews, R. C. O., 'The Theory of Growth: A Survey', *Economic Journal*, 1964.

Haig, B. D., 'Do New Factories Embody Best Practice Technology? – A Comment', *Economic Journal*, 1975.

Harcourt, G. C., *Some Cambridge Controversies in the Theory of Capital*, Cambridge University Press, 1972.

Haveman, R. and DeBartolo, G., 'The Revenue Maximizing Oligopoly Model', *American Economic Review*, 1968.

Heathfield, D. F., 'The Measurement of Capital Usage Using Electricity Consumption Data for the UK', *Journal of the Royal Statistical Society*, 1972a.

Heathfield, D., 'Factor Substitution: Some Empirical Results for Six UK Manufacturing Industries', Discussion Paper No. 7205, Department of Economics, Southampton University, 1972b.

Helps, I. G., 'Forecasting Manpower: A Review of Some Models Used for Forecasting Changes in Total Employment at National and Sectoral Level', Working Paper National Economic Development Office, 1974.

Hildebrand, G. H. and Liu, I. C., *Manufacturing Production Functions in the US, 1957*, New York State School of Industrial and Labour Relations, 1965.

*Historical Abstract of Labour Statistics*, Department of Employment.

Houthakker, H. S., 'The Pareto Distribution and the Cobb–Douglas Production Function in Activity Analysis', *Review of Economic Studies*, 1955–56.

*Industrial Trends*, Confederation of British Industries.

Johansen, L., 'Substitution versus Fixed Production Coefficients in the Theory of Economic Growth: A Synthesis', *Econometrica*, 1959.

Johansen, L., 'A Method for Separating the Effects of Capital Accumulation and

Shifts in Production Functions upon Growth in Labour Productivity', *Economic Journal*, 1961.

Johansen, L., *Production Functions – An Integration of Micro and Macro, Short-Run and Long-Run Aspects*, North Holland, Amsterdam 1972.

Kaldor, N., 'A Model of Economic Growth', *Economic Journal*, 1957.

Kamien, M. I. and Swartz, N. L., 'Timing of Innovations Under Rivalry', *Econometrica*, 1972.

Klein, L. R., *An Introduction to Econometrics*, Prentice Hall, Englewood Cliffs, NJ 1962.

Kmenta, J., 'On the Estimation of the CES Production Function', *International Economic Review*, vol. 8, no. 2, 1967.

Kurz, M. and Manne, A. S., 'Engineering Estimates of Capital Labor Substitution in Metal Machining', *American Economic Review*, 1963.

*Labour Yearbook*, Department of Employment.

Lave, L. B., *Technological Change: Its Conception and Measurement*, Prentice Hall, Englewood Cliffs, NJ, 1966.

Layard, P. R. G., Sargan, J. D., Ager, M. E. and Jones, D. J., *Qualified Manpower and Economic Performance*, Allen Lane, The Penguin Press, 1971.

Leech, D., 'A Note on Testing the Error Specification in Non-Linear Regression', *Econometrica*, 1975.

Liebenstein, H., 'Allocative Efficiency Versus X-Efficiency', *American Economic Review*, 1966.

Liebenstein, H., 'Organizational or Frictional Equilibria, X-Efficiency, and the Rate of Innovation', *Quarterly Journal of Economics*, 1969.

Leontief, W. W., 'A Note on the Interrelation of Subsets of Independent Variables of a Continuous Function with Continuous First Derivatives', *Bulletin of the American Mathematical Society*, 1947.

Leontie , W. W., 'Introduction to the Theory of the Internal Structure of Functional Relationships', *Econometrica*, 1947.

Lindley, R., 'The Demand for Apprentice Recruits by the Engineering Industry, 1951–71', *Scottish Journal of Political Economy*, 1975.

Lipsey, R. G., 'Structural and Deficient Demand Unemployment Reconsidered', in A. M. Ross (ed.), *Employment Policy and the Labour Market*, University of California Press, 1965.

Machlup, F., 'The Production and Distribution of Knowledge in the US', in *The Rate and Direction of Inventive Activity: Economic and Social Factors*, Princeton University Press, 1962.

Markowitz, H. M. and Rowe, A. J., 'A Machine Tool Substitution Analysis', in *Studies in Process Analysis*, Cowles Foundation, 1961.

Marris, R., 'An Introduction to Theories of Corporate Growth', in R. Marris and A. Woods (eds), *The Corporate Economy*, Macmillan, London, 1971.

Mayor, T. H., 'Some theoretical difficulties in the estimation of the elasticity of substitution from cross-sectional data', *Western Economic Journal*, 1969.

*Ministry of Labour Gazette* (later the *Department of Employment Gazette*).

Moody, C. E., 'The Measurement of Capital Services by Electrical Energy', *Bulletin of Economic Research*, 1974.

Mueller, D. C., 'The Firm's Decision Process: An Econometric Investigation', *Quarterly Journal of Economics*, 1967.

Nadiri, M. I. and Rosen, S., 'Inter-related Factor Demand Functions', *American Economic Review*, 1968.

National Board for Prices and Incomes, Chairman A. Jones, Cmnd. 4554, HMSO, 1970.

Nelson, P. R., 'Technical Change and Growth Accounting', Paper delivered at the Royal Economic Society Conference on Technical Progress, 1973.

Nerlove, M., *Estimation and Identification of Cobb–Douglas Production Functions*, North Holland, Amsterdam 1966.

*New Earnings Survey*, Department of Employment.

Nordhaus, W. D., *Invention, Growth and Welfare*, Massachusetts Institute of Technology Press, 1969.

Nordhaus, W. D., 'Some Sceptical Thoughts on the Theory of Induced Innovation', *Quarterly Journal of Economics*, 1973.

Park, S. T., 'Bounded Substitution, Fixed Proportions and Economic Growth', *Yale Economic Essays*, 1966.

Phelps, E. S., 'The New View of Investment', *Quarterly Journal of Economics*, 1962.

Phelps, E. S., *Golden Rules of Economic Growth*, W. W. Norton & Co., New York 1966.

Phillips, A., 'The Variation in Technical Coefficients in the Anti-Friction Bearing Industry', *Econometrica*, 1955.

Piore, M. J., 'The Impact of the Labour Market upon the Design and Selection of Productive Techniques within the Manufacturing Plant', *Quarterly Journal of Economics*, 1968.

Pyatt, F. G., 'A Measure of Capital', *Review of Economic Studies*, 1963.

Pyatt, F. G., 'A Production Functional Model', P. E. Hart et al. (eds), *Econometric Analysis for Economic Planning*, Butterworth, London 1964a.

Pyatt, F. G., *Capital Output and Employment, 1948–60*, in the series 'A Programme for Growth', Chapman and Hall, London 1964b.

Robinson, J., 'The Production Function and the Theory of Capital', *Review of Economic Studies*, 1953–54.

Robinson, J., 'Capital Theory up to date', *Canadian Journal of Economics*, 1970.

Robinson, J., *Economic Heresies: Some Old-Fashioned Questions in Economic Theory*, Basic Books, New York 1971.

Ruttan, V., 'Usher and Schumpeter on Invention, Innovation and Technological Change', *Quarterly Journal of Economics*, 1959.

Salter, W. E. G., *Productivity and Technical Change*, Cambridge University Press, 1966.

Samuelson, P. A., 'Parable and Realism in Capital Theory: The Surrogate Production Function', *Review of Economic Studies*, 1962.

Sandmeyer, R. L., 'Baumol's Sales Maximization Model', *American Economic Review*, 1964.

Sato, K., 'The Neoclassical Postulate and the Technology Frontier in Capital Theory', *Quarterly Journal of Economics*, 1974.

Sawyer, M. C., 'Concentration in British Manufacturing Industry', *Oxford Economic Papers*, 1971.

Schmookler, J., *Invention and Economic Growth*, Harvard University Press, 1966.

Senker, P. and Huggett, C., 'Technology and Manpower in the UK Engineering Industry', Occasional Paper No. 3, Engineering Industry Training Board, 1973.

Senker, P., Huggett, C., Bell, M. and Sciberras, E., 'Technological Change, Structural Change and Manpower in the UK Toolmaking Industry', Occasional Paper, Science Policy Research Unit, Sussex University, 1975.

Sevaldson, P., 'Changes in Input–Output Coefficients', in T. Barna (ed.), *Structural Interdependence and Economic Development*, Macmillan, London, 1963.

Simon, H. A., 'Theories of decision-making in economics and the behavioral sciences', *American Economic Review*, 1959.

Steele, L., 'Loyalty', in D. Allison (ed.), *The R & D Game*, Massachusetts Institution of Technology Press, 1969.

Stone, R., *Input–Output Relationships 1954–66*, in the series 'A Programme for Growth', Chapman and Hall, London, 1963.

Solow, R. M., 'The Production Function and the Theory of Capital', *Review of Economic Studies*, 1956.

Solow, R. M., 'Technical Change and the Aggregate Production Function', *Review of Economic Studies*, 1957.

Solow, R. M., 'Investment and Technical Progress', in K. J. Arrow (ed.) *Mathematical Methods in the Social Sciences*, Stanford University Press, 1960.

Solow, R. M., 'Review of Capital and Growth', *American Economic Review*, 1966.

Solow, R. M., 'The Production Function and the Theory of Capital', *Review of Economic Studies*, Taylor, 1967.

Svennilson, I., 'Economic Growth and Technical Progress: An Essay in Sequence Analysis', in *The Residual Factor and Economic Growth*, Organisation for Economic Cooperation and Development, Paris, 1964.

Taylor, J., 'A Surrogate for Regional Estimates of Capital Stock', *Bulletin of Economic Research*, 1967.

Wabe, J. S., 'Output and Employment', in J. S. Wabe et al., 'Manpower Forecasting for the Engineering Industry', Occasional Paper No. 4, Engineering Industry Training Board, 1974.

Wallander, J., *Verkstadsindustriens Maskinkapital*, Swedish Institute of Industrial Research, Stockholm 1962.

Wan, H. Y., *Economic Growth*, Harcourt, Brace, Jovanovich, New York 1971.

Wildsmith, J. R., *Managerial Theories of the Firm*, Martin Robertson, 1973.

Williams, B. R., *Technology, Investment and Growth*, Chapman and Hall, London 1967.

Williamson, O. E., *Corporate Control and Business Behaviour*, Prentice Hall, 1970.

Wrigley, K. J., 'Production Models and Time Trends of Input–Output Coefficients', in F. W. Gossling (ed.), *Input–Output in the United Kingdom*, Frank Cass and Co., London 1970.

# Index

# The author

Derek Bosworth took his BA at Lanchester Polytechnic and his MA at Warwick University, where he worked with the Manpower Unit at the CIEBR. Now a Lecturer in Industrial Economics at the University of Loughborough, he still maintains his interest in the Manpower Unit at Warwick.

# Other SAXON HOUSE Publications

| | |
|---|---|
| Hodges, M. | *Multinational corporations and national governments* |
| Liggins, D. | *National economic planning in France* |
| Friedly, P. H. | *National policy responses to urban growth* |
| Madelin, H. | *Oil and politics* |
| Tilford, R. (ed.) | *The Ostpolitik and political change in Germany* |
| Friedrichs, J., H. Ludtke | *Participant observation* |
| Fitzmaurice, J. | *The party groups in the European parliament* |
| Brown, J., G. Howes (eds) | *The police and the community* |
| Lang, R. W. | *The politics of drugs* |
| Denton, F. T., B. G. Spencer | *Population and the economy* |
| Dickinson, J. P. (ed.) | *Portfolio analysis* |
| Wilson, D. J. | *Power and party bureaucracy in Britain* |
| Wabe, J. S. | *Problems in manpower forecasting* |
| Willis, K. G. | *Problems in migration analysis* |
| Farnsworth, R. A. | *Productivity and law* |
| Shepherd, R. J. | *Public opinion and European integration* |
| Richardson, H. W. | *Regional development policy and planning in Spain* |
| Sant, M. (ed.) | *Regional policy and planning for Europe* |
| Thorpe, D. (ed.) | *Research into retailing and distribution* |
| Dickinson, J. P. | *Risk and uncertainty in accounting and finance* |
| Hey, R. D., T. D. Davies (eds) | *Science, technology and environmental management* |
| Britton, D. K., B. Hill | *Size and efficiency in farming* |
| Buchholz, E., et al | *Socialist criminology* |
| Paterson, W. E. | *The SPD and European integration* |
| Blohm, H., K. Steinbuch (eds) | *Technological forecasting in practice* |
| Piepe, A., et al | *Television and the working class* |
| Goodhardt, G. J., et al | *The television audience* |
| May, T. C. | *Trade unions and pressure group politics* |
| Labini, P. S. | *Trade unions, inflation and productivity* |
| Casadio, G. P. | *Transatlantic trade* |
| Whitehead, C. M. E. | *The U.K. housing market* |
| Balfour, C. | *Unions and the law* |

WITHDRAWN
UST
Libraries

ANWESCHT
...
L ......